CHINA'S SCIENTIFIC POLICIES

AEI-Hoover
policy studies

The studies in this series are issued jointly
by the American Enterprise Institute
for Public Policy Research and the Hoover
Institution on War, Revolution and Peace.
They are designed to focus on
policy problems of current and future interest,
to set forth the factors underlying
these problems and to evaluate
courses of action available to policy makers.
The views expressed in these studies
are those of the authors and do not necessarily
reflect the views of the staff, officers
or members of the governing boards of
AEI or the Hoover Institution.

CHINA'S SCIENTIFIC POLICIES

Implications for international cooperation

Charles P. Ridley

American Enterprise Institute for Public Policy Research
Washington, D. C.

Hoover Institution on War, Revolution and Peace
Stanford University, Stanford, California

AEI-Hoover Policy Study 20, October 1976
(Hoover Institution Studies 50)

ISBN 0-8447-3222-2
Library of Congress Catalog Card No. 76-40544

Printed in United States of America

Contents

Introduction

The aim of this study is to assess the effects of the Cultural Revolution, which got under way in 1966, on the course of scientific development in China and to arrive at some tentative conclusions concerning the prospects for scientific exchange and cooperation between China and the United States. It is hoped that the information presented here will be of assistance to scientists who might be contemplating joint ventures with their Chinese counterparts.

While it is difficult in practice to draw a strict line between science and technology, the central concern of this study is the development of the fundamental scientific disciplines comprising the biological, medical, and physical sciences. Thus, our perspective here may be of greater relevance to research scientists in academic, industrial, or governmental institutions than to those engaged in the technological application of scientific discoveries.

This assessment of the state of the various scientific disciplines in China is based primarily on the available published literature that was produced from the time publication resumed in 1972 until July 1974. It is clear, however, that there is much research in progress in China that is not being reported in the major journals. Indeed, visitors to China have indicated that many scientists express reluctance to rush into print. In addition, there are apparently a number of local university journals in publication that have not been available outside China.

Therefore, our assessments are based, and can only be based, on incomplete information. On the other hand, the information we have is far more complete than a statistical sampling and should be highly representative of the proportion of effort being devoted to and the degree of specialization in any given discipline.

1

The policy of the Chinese government toward the sciences can be summed up briefly. It places heavy emphasis on applied research that can contribute directly to the development of agriculture and industry, to the general welfare of the people, and to defense, although little literature on defense is available. There is also a strong tendency to opt for direct labor-intensive approaches to solving certain types of problems rather than to rely on time-consuming basic studies of uncertain outcome. This approach is adopted at the expense of "basic" or nonutilitarian research; it implies, as one Chinese slogan tells us, the intention to rely on the results of basic research done in other countries.

A number of facets of Chinese policy toward the sciences strike the outsider as unique. One of these is the tendency to adapt and apply as much of the traditional Chinese scientific heritage as possible. This trend is particularly evident in medicine, as well as in such fields as geology where it has led to the study and use of detailed records kept over the course of Chinese history. Perhaps the most unique and striking feature of Chinese scientific policy, however, has been the attempt to involve the masses in scientific experimentation, particularly in such fields as agriculture, public health, and weather and earthquake prediction, where large quantities of raw data must be gathered and tested on a broad scale.

Closely related to these developments is the policy of the Chinese government toward the scientists themselves. The so-called mass experimentation movement implies a policy of integrating research scientists with the masses. If Chinese reports are to be taken at face value, considerable numbers of scientists have left their laboratories in both major and minor research institutes to work for varying periods of time with, for example, farmers, directing and conducting experiments and seeking out the practical knowledge of the farmers to guide them in setting and solving research problems.

The major thrust of government action toward the scientists has been to "reeducate" them in order to eliminate "bourgeois" or "revisionist" attitudes toward science and the purposes of scientific research. This has meant the attempt to eliminate the belief in science for science's sake and to develop among scientists the view that science is a utilitarian vehicle for serving "socialist construction" and the concrete needs of the people. It has also been part of an attempt to prevent the rise of the scientists as an elite class, which has happened in the Soviet Union.

2

It is not clear to what extent all scientists have been subjected to reeducation, but there is a good possibility that scientists in certain high-priority fields such as nuclear physics, missile research, and military research in general may have been largely shielded from the series of movements for political education or indoctrination that has been conducted over the past several years. This, however, is purely a matter of speculation.

In general, these policies toward the sciences reflect the overall narrowing of policy toward intellectual expression that has been manifested since the Cultural Revolution. The character of these policies was given official expression in the new constitution of the People's Republic of China which was adopted at the Fourth National People's Congress in Peking in January 1975. While article ninety-five of the 1954 constitution spoke of the "freedom of citizens to engage in scientific research, literary and artistic creation and other cultural pursuits," article twelve of the new constitution is an explicit expression of the newer, more restrictive orientation: "The proletariat must exercise all-round dictatorship over the bourgeoisie in the superstructure, including all spheres of culture. Culture and education, literature and art, physical education, health work and scientific research must all serve proletarian politics, serve the workers, peasants and soldiers, and be combined with productive labor." As the following pages show, it is just such a basic policy that has been applied to the sciences.

It should be evident that these policies toward the sciences and scientists have considerable implications for cooperative programs between American and Chinese scientists, both in terms of the kinds of joint research projects that might be attempted and in terms of relationships at the everyday working level. These topics are explored in greater detail in the pages that follow.

It should also be clear from these remarks that we will be looking at the workings of science in a society that takes a radically different and far more utilitarian view of the purposes of science than that traditionally prevailing in the West. The Chinese approach stands in sharp contrast to the Western tradition of science for science's sake, by virtue of which scientists dedicated to seeking out the principles of the natural world have followed their personal interests guided by the internal logic of their disciplines and very often with little regard to the social utility of their work.

While official Chinese policy makers have taken a stance far more utilitarian than that adopted even in the Soviet Union at a comparable stage in the course of its political development, much of what has been happening in the sciences in China should be of interest to American scientists from a purely political standpoint. This should be particularly true at a time when the sciences have become increasingly vital to national development and defense and when decisions on funding of research projects have consequently come more and more under the surveillance of political figures who are often not sympathetic to, nor competent to judge the merits of, research in particular fields.

It is in this context that China is of particular interest, for China is a nation in which, to use a Chinese phrase, "politics has taken command" of the sciences in a much more obvious and extreme way than has occurred in Western societies. As Robert Heilbroner has suggested, in the face of the grave problems now facing the world, the days of free intellectual inquiry may be numbered as governments take on ever greater powers to deal with the technological and political crises waiting in the wings or already upon us.[1] Because of the extreme position the Chinese have adopted, the treatment of the sciences and scientists in China may not be the model of the future for governments in the democracies, yet the Chinese experience may be an indication of a general trend. Indeed, as Salomon has indicated, the complexity of the scientific and technological problems facing governments today and the costliness of pursuing solutions to them tend to increase the level of political control over scientific work, irrespective of national ideology.[2]

The conflict, then, is one in which the lines are clearly drawn: the right of the scientist to pursue his own interests versus the right of society to determine what tasks the scientist should undertake. The Chinese have consciously chosen the latter alternative, while the scientific community in the United States is moving with varying degrees of self-awareness toward the same end, impelled by a complex of circumstances that may be equally inexorable.

The choice that the Chinese have made gives us pause to reflect on what the relationship between the sciences and society ought to be as we enter a new era in the history of mankind. Decisions on scientific policy have become too important to human welfare to leave to the scientists and far too complex to entrust to the judgment of politicians.

---

[1] Robert L. Heilbroner, *An Inquiry into the Human Prospect* (New York: W. W. Norton and Co., 1974), p. 26.
[2] Jean-Jacques Salomon, *Science and Politics,* trans. Noël Lindsay (Cambridge: M.I.T. Press, 1973), pp. xviii–xix.

4

1
Science in Society
since the Cultural Revolution

The sciences are vital to the future of modern China. When China's leaders look about them, they see a wide range of problems, many of which are dependent for their solution on the application of scientific knowledge. Internally, they are faced with the problems of feeding and maintaining the health of a huge population and of developing a self-sufficient industrial base. Essential to these tasks is a rational allocation of manpower in the agricultural, biological, medical, and earth sciences, and in such fields as chemistry. From an international standpoint, China must develop sophisticated modern military systems in order to take its place as a major world power as well as to secure its safety against its historical enemy, the Soviet Union, with which it shares a long and fragile border. China must also strengthen its position in relation to that uncertain factor in the international equation, the United States. This means the development of programs of research on atomic energy, guided missiles, and possibly spacecraft, in which a variety of disciplines, from physics and mathematics to astronomy and metallurgy, play important parts. Clearly, these are goals that cannot be attained without centralized planning for scientific development.

When we look at the manner in which the sciences are organized in China, we discover that general planning for research occurs at the highest levels of government. At the top of the hierarchy is the State Council of the People's Republic of China, which formulates the State Plan that covers scientific endeavors and to which the Chinese Academy of Sciences (CAS), which includes the major research organizations in China, is subordinate. Since the founding of the People's Republic of China in 1949, there have been a number of shifts in the degree of autonomy enjoyed by the institutes of the Chinese Academy of

Sciences in setting research projects.[1] In the last few years in particular scientists and technicians appear to have surrendered more and more of their control over the content of research, as the administrative and academic affairs of the institutes have come under the control of "revolutionary committees." These committees are composed of a "three-in-one combination" of cadres, workers and technicians, and "progressive" intellectuals.[2] Similar committees oversee research at other institutes and in the universities. The Scientific and Technical Association, which has been responsible for inviting and hosting foreign visitors, also plays a significant although not fully understood role in scientific leadership, perhaps serving as a watchdog organization concerned with the execution of scientific plans.

It is through such structures, which are essentially intrusions of the political sector into the scientific community, that policy decisions affecting the sciences are implemented. Control over the sciences by these means has grown substantially since 1966, a year that marks a major turning point in policy toward the sciences.

Although Chinese scientists had concerned themselves almost entirely with applied research during the first decade after 1949, the first half of the 1960s witnessed a rise in the quantity and in the level of sophistication of research in many fields, in particular biochemistry and organic chemistry. During this period scientists seemed to have a more or less free rein over the direction their studies were taking, and many of them engaged in basic research.

What might be thought of as the natural progression of development within individual scientific disciplines was brought to a halt through the intervention of the Cultural Revolution, a complex movement combining both political and cultural goals that arose in 1966. While its initial aim was undoubtedly political—that of purging Liu Shao-ch'i and his followers, who were accused of "taking the capitalist road"—the Cultural Revolution also served as a vehicle for mass movements intended to destroy any vestiges of the traditional culture. It was in essence a massive attempt to turn the country around, and one of its targets was scientific research. Research institutes as well as educational institutions at all levels were closed as professors and scientists were subjected to programs of reeducation and attempts were

---

[1] For a thorough study of the organization of the sciences in China, see Richard P. Suttmeier, *Research and Revolution: Science Policy and Societal Change in China* (Lexington, Mass.: Lexington Books, 1974).
[2] Ibid., p. 104.

6

made to ferret out those who were advocating and pursuing a "revisionist line" in scientific research. The publication of scientific journals ceased, not to resume until 1972.

The attack on the sciences was intended to make way for a new policy giving emphasis to applied research, the results of which would be of direct service to the people and to national construction. In the light of the policy of "taking agriculture as the foundation" of national development, this shift in emphasis clearly implied that research contributing to agricultural development would be accorded a high priority. In practice, it has also implied a policy of bringing laboratory scientists into closer contact with field conditions in the countryside and a concomitant policy of popularization of scientific knowledge and methods.

Since another key factor in development is the general level of health of a population, it is not surprising that medical research and the medical sciences in general also came under close scrutiny. Here too there has been a major policy shift away from basic research, which is often costly, time-consuming, and without immediate practical benefits, to approaches aimed at the prevention of disease. The implementation of such policies obviously necessitated severe dislocations in research programs and, as we shall note, met with resistance from some scientists.

Since one of our concerns here is the outlook for scientific cooperation and exchange between China and the United States, it is important to assess both the manner in which control of the sciences has been effected and the extent to which it can be exercised in China. The experience of the Cultural Revolution is an extreme example of the power of the political over the scientific sector and an indication of how the course of scientific research can be interrupted and diverted as a result of political considerations.

Before turning to this topic, however, it may be helpful to consider the problem of the sciences from the perspective of China's political leaders. The sciences, in fact, present them with a serious, basically ideological dilemma. The sciences are clearly essential. However, the modern sciences are of Western origin, and most of China's senior scientists were trained in either Europe or the United States. It is this nucleus of Western-trained scientists that has been responsible for developing the scientific disciplines to the level they presently enjoy in China. This in itself would not be a problem were it not for the facts that the scientific disciplines are international in orientation and that

7

each has a tendency to develop according to its own internal logic. Traditionally, Western scientists have studied natural phenomena because of their intrinsic interest and because of the challenge and excitement of trying to unlock the mysteries of nature, without necessarily concerning themselves with practical applications.

As a result, there is an inevitable tension between Western-trained scientists and the political leaders, whose interests are purely practical and who wish to incorporate the philosophically alien Western sciences into the framework of Marxist-Leninist-Maoist ideology. China's leaders must depend on these same, perhaps politically unreliable, scientists to train future generations of scientists, thus running some risk of the latter being contaminated by an alien scientific ideology. Within the ranks of the scientists, there are two distinct major groups, those trained in the West and perhaps tainted with a "bourgeois world view," and those trained in China, who passed their formative years under the new regime and thus are more apt to be in harmony with the utilitarian scientific philosophy. As a consequence of the ideological and philosophical difference between Western science and Chinese views and the basically conflicting standpoints of the Western-trained scientists and the political sector, China's political leaders have felt called upon to exert considerable force to tame the scientists and to redirect the course of scientific research.

For purposes of analysis, the shift in China's scientific policy can be divided into three stages: an initial stage in which there was an indirect call for a change of policy, the dissolution of the research community, and the reconstitution of the research community under new structures of control and with new goals.

Indirect Calls for a Change in Policy

With the benefit of hindsight, it is clear that there were broad hints of impending change in the late winter and early spring of 1966. During that period a considerable number of articles linking politics and research appeared in Chinese scientific and medical journals. Most of these articles dealt with three major themes: the direction and goals of research, the methodology of research, and personal attitudes toward research. Their apparent aim was to stimulate China's research workers to rethink these topics. The better part of these articles appeared in journals devoted to agriculture and medicine, the very areas in which some of the greatest changes were to take place.

8

One such article, an editorial in the March 1966 issue of *Chinese Agricultural Science* (*Chung-kuo Nung-yeh K'o-hsüeh*), dealt primarily with the attitudes of agricultural scientists to work in demonstration fields. Compared to the direct attacks to be made later in the Cultural Revolution, it was mild and merely suggestive.

How does science emerge from the demonstration fields? One of the determining conditions is whether scientific research is closely integrated with the agricultural production of a region. Whenever, under the Party Committee of a region, fulfillment of current production is taken as its major mission and problems of production urgently requiring solution are taken up as topics of research, then production in the region is enhanced and scientific research develops. . . . The party policies of "uniting theory with practice" and of "scientific research serving production" have come to be supported by the greater majority of workers in agricultural technology. However, among the ranks of our nation's workers in agricultural science and technology there still exists a view of research and a research working style that are divorced from production, divorced from practice, and divorced from the masses. Therefore, even though some comrades have come down from their towers and out from their courtyards, they still have not been able to serve production in the demonstration fields completely and thoroughly. The solution to this problem is not merely a question of working methods but is first a question of embracing a proletarian, dialectical materialist world outlook.[3]

The editorialist goes on to state that it is only those who hold a proletarian outlook and who are firm about casting out old research methods who can succeed in raising the level of agricultural production and in promoting agricultural science. Then he turns to those who have not followed such a course:

But those comrades who hold a bourgeois world view do not understand that agricultural scientific theory comes primarily from the practice of production and do not comprehend the dialectical relationship between popularization and elevation, holding that all they can do in the demonstration fields is carry out popularization but that they cannot produce science. Thus although they were compelled by circumstances to go down to the demonstration fields, they are not able to launch into work setting out from current production but are still shut

---

[3] "We Still Have to Start Talking from Ideology," *Chung-kuo Nung-yeh K'o-hsüeh* [Chinese agricultural science], no. 3 (March 1966), p. 49 (author's translation).

up in their laboratories dealing with vials and jars. From the start the masses do not welcome them, they are of no assistance to production, and there is no way in which they can further scientific research.

This statement can certainly be taken as a call for agricultural scientists to work more closely with the farmers and to direct their research toward solving practical agricultural problems.

It is, however, in an editorial in the *Chinese Journal of Internal Medicine* (*Chung-hua Nei-k'o Tsa-chih*) entitled "Raise High the Great Red Flag of the Thought of Mao Tse-tung and Continue to Beat Out Our Own Path in the Struggle against Hepatitis" that we find the first concrete expression of a number of themes that were to assume increasing importance as the Cultural Revolution wore on. The writer indicates that, although a great deal of progress has been made in the struggle against hepatitis, serious problems still remain regarding its diagnosis, prevention, and treatment. He then says:

> If we are to complete this mission and batter down this fortress we must give prominence to politics, and, arming our minds with the thought of Mao Tse-tung, use dialectical materialism as a research method, further strengthen solidarity and cooperation between Chinese [traditional] medicine and Western medicine, follow the mass line, make a large effort at cooperation, give play to a creative spirit and resolve to take a national course of our own.[4]

In the writer's view, this means grasping three primary "links": (1) "specifying the direction of service and grasping the key points of research," (2) "opposing metaphysical and encouraging dialectical materialist research methods," and (3) "thoroughly mobilizing the masses and engaging in a common struggle against hepatitis." He elaborates on the first point as follows:

> Hepatitis is one of the commonly seen diseases that has serious effects on the health and labor productivity of the laboring people. Anyone who is a revolutionary medical worker can hardly take a light view of it. We must, with deep class feeling and by every means and without turning from the task, search for effective measures to prevent this disease in order to serve the workers, peasants and soldiers

---

[4] "Raise High the Great Red Flag of the Thought of Mao Tse-tung and Continue to Beat Out Our Own Path in the Struggle against Hepatitis," *Chung-hua Nei-k'o Tsa-chih* [Chinese journal of internal medicine], vol. 14, no. 4 (April 1966), p. 232 (author's translation).

and in order to serve the people. For this reason, the basic purpose of our research on hepatitis is to eliminate hepatitis, to strengthen the physical constitution of the people, to preserve the labor force, to promote production, and to hasten socialist construction. Beyond these, we ought perhaps to have other purposes. However, in hepatitis research in the past, a great deal of emphasis was placed on diagnosis and experimental research while there was comparatively less work on its prevention and cure. This was clearly incorrect.

The writer goes on to stress the importance of freeing people from this illness so that they will be able to devote themselves to the "socialist revolution and socialist construction." He then returns to the direction of research:

If we medical workers, in the face of these pressing demands on the part of our own class brothers, do not strive to conduct research on methods of preventing hepatitis, this is not in the least a technical problem but is rather a problem of direction. We emphasize putting the key point of scientific research on hepatitis on the aspects of prevention and treatment. This is a point that we should grasp aggressively. To be sure, this is not equivalent to not concerning ourselves with diagnosis, experimental research, and other research.

He goes on to discuss methodology, insisting on the use of dialectical materialism rather than metaphysical approaches in research, rejecting "foreign and old models" while absorbing foreign techniques and experiences in a spirit of self-reliance and independent creativity. One point that he makes on the topic of methodology amounts to a repudiation of statistical methods of analysis, for he remarks that a researcher "should not be satisfied with a percentage of average numbers of gains but must uphold the principle of concrete analysis of concrete problems."

In regard to his third point, or "link," the author quotes Mao—"The popular masses have unlimited creative capacity"—and stresses the point that "it is difficult to achieve anything merely by relying on a small number of persons working in isolation." Instead he calls for a "policy of triple alliance between the leaders, the specialists, and the masses," cooperating to annihilate the disease.

Such were the themes that appeared just prior to the Cultural Revolution. At that time there was no hint that they amounted to anything more than attempts at persuasion similar to past exhortations. But as later events were to show, they foreshadowed the deep and thorough change in the orientation of the sciences away from basic research that was to be enforced by the Cultural Revolution.

The Attack on the
Scientific Research Community

While it would be impossible in a short space to describe the assault on the sciences in detail, it is important to take note of its key themes both because of its actual influence and because of its value as evidence of the actual and potential power that the political sector wields over scientists and research institutions.

The first blow to strike the Chinese scientific community—and that which impressed the outside world most forcefully—was the suspension of publication of scientific journals. This was preceded in the late spring of 1966 by an increase in the political content of the journals, illustrated by the paper quoted above on hepatitis research. By June, however, as the Cultural Revolution was getting under way in earnest, reports on research began to give way to reprints of articles from the *People's Daily* (*Jen-min Jih-pao*) and the *Liberation Army Daily* (*Chieh-fang Jih-pao*) relating to the Cultural Revolution. The June issue of the *Acta Botanica Sinica,* for example, devoted thirty-six pages to such reprints and to articles calling for active participation in the Cultural Revolution. Most journals stopped publication with their June issues, although the *Acta Entomologica Sinica* held out through August. As far as we know, most scientific research came to a halt at that time as the entire nation plunged into a period of intense political turmoil.

It was during the summer of 1967, however, that the attack on the sciences began to move into high gear. Its targets were those within the world of scientific research who were "taking the capitalist road" or advocating the "revisionist line in research." What this meant can be seen from the "repudiation" of two of China's leading political figures, Peng Te-huai and Lo Jui-ching, in August 1967 for their part as "agents of China's Khrushchev" (that is, of Liu Shao-ch'i) in "pushing the counterrevolutionary revisionist line in national defense scientific research institutes and departments." The two men were accused of opposing the "correct principle" for scientific research on national defense put forth by Mao and Vice-Chairman Lin Piao (later to run into trouble himself), who advocated a policy of "going all out, aiming high, and being determined by self-reliance and hard work to catch up with

12

and surpass the most advanced scientific levels in the world." Part of the accusation against them read as follows:

> They opposed to the utmost Chairman Mao's principle of striving vigorously to build up the might and prosperity of the country by relying on our own strength. They willingly played the role of lackeys of U. S. imperialism and Soviet revisionism, and made great efforts to peddle and carry out the principle of slavishness, of capitulation to U. S. imperialism and Soviet revisionism. They spread such capitulationist nonsense as "we can rely on the Soviet Union for long-range guided missiles" and "when it is getting dark in the east, it is getting bright in the west," meaning "we can buy some weapons from the capitalist countries," and so on. All this was in a vain attempt to pull the national defense scientific research of our great socialist country back to the old path of a colony or semicolony. They frenziedly opposed the great strategic idea of "catching up and surpassing" put forward by Chairman Mao, and viciously slandered the effort to scale the heights of national defense science as "overreaching oneself." Thus they made up their minds to crawl along the path of "capitalism and revisionism."[5]

Thus, at the highest level the attack was an expression of dissatisfaction with the "revisionist" policy of relying too heavily on the outside world in the sphere of national defense research. In essence, it was a call to go it alone, a call for self-reliance in defense technology similar to that voiced earlier in medical research. As the record following the Cultural Revolution and the development of missiles by the Chinese makes clear, self-reliance has become a key pillar of Chinese policy toward the sciences.

In terms of general scientific research, as opposed to defense research, the overall policy was to bring the content of research more closely into line with the concrete needs of the people and of development. To bring about this end, the research institutes of the Chinese Academy of Sciences became far more politicized than they had ever been before.

A key event in the political subjugation of the Chinese Academy of Sciences was the formal inauguration of a body known as the Revolutionary Committee of the Chinese Academy of Sciences on 30 July 1967 in the Great Hall of the People. Both Premier Chou En-lai and Kuo Mo-jo, chairman of the Chinese Academy of Sciences, were

---

[5] NCNA International Service, 27 August 1967, Peking.

present.[6] Chou En-lai, in his speech before the academy, expressed the belief that the inauguration of the Revolutionary Committee was an indication that

> the Chinese Academy of Sciences will be turned into a red, red great school of Mao Tse-tung's thought and will follow a course pointed out by Chairman Mao to catch up with and surpass world levels in science and technology, and come forward with the most advanced sciences and technology in the world.[7]

Premier Chou was followed by Wang Hsi-peng of the Revolutionary Committee of the Chinese Academy of Sciences, who dealt more specifically with the role of the Revolutionary Committee in the academy:

> The birth of the Revolutionary Committee of the Chinese Academy of Sciences marks a decisive victory won by the proletarian revolutionaries of the Chinese Academy of Sciences in their struggle for seizing power from the handful of party persons in authority taking the capitalist road, a decisive victory of Chairman Mao's revolutionary line in the Chinese Academy of Sciences, and the entry into a new stage of the Great Proletarian Cultural Revolution in the Chinese Academy of Sciences.[8]

Wang went on to suggest "ten tasks" that faced the "proletarian revolutionaries" in the academy:

> Bring about a new upsurge in the creative study and application of Chairman Mao's works in the course of carrying out the large-scale repudiation campaign in order to elevate the campaign to a new level;
>
> Consolidate and develop the revolutionary great alliances and the three-way alliances during this campaign;
>
> Promote the struggle-repudiation-reform campaign in the whole academy;
>
> Sincerely change the style of work of the leadership;
>
> Consolidate the proletarian dictatorship;
>
> Practice economy in pursuing the revolution in response to great leader Chairman Mao's call;
>
> Grasp the revolution and stimulate production;

---

[6] NCNA Domestic Service, 2 August 1967, Peking.
[7] Peking Domestic Service, 2 August 1967.
[8] Ibid.

Oppose all the old bureaucratic practices;

Streamline and revolutionize all organizations;

Catch up with and surpass world levels in scientific and research work.[9]

While it is not clear precisely what all of these statements meant, it is clear that there was considerable strife and commotion within the institutes of the academy at this time. It was announced later, in fact, that there had been, since May 1967, a "revolutionary repudiation campaign" within the academy, which had launched "ferocious attacks" against "China's Khrushchev [Liu Shao-ch'i] and his agents in the Chinese Academy of Sciences."[10]

Whatever the rhetoric, however, the battle was about control of the content and direction of scientific research. What was being attacked by the political leaders of the Cultural Revolution was the "poisonous influence" of the "revisionist line in scientific research"—the policy of encouraging research not directly concerned with practical, everyday problems. The revisionist line was denounced as "divorced from proletarian politics, from practical work, and from the workers, peasants and soldiers."[11] Thus China's political leaders set about on the contradictory course of attempting to "catch up with and surpass world levels in scientific and research work" while turning their scientists away from fundamental and toward utilitarian research.

It appears that the task of combating the revisionist line occupied a considerable period of time, and reports show that it continued into 1969. The agents for reform within the research institutes were very often groups known as "Mao Tse-tung worker thought propaganda teams," which were described as militant groups of workers, peasants and soldiers, and "People's Liberation Army [PLA] thought propaganda teams." These groups, which were reported to have gone into scientific research institutes throughout China, existed for the purpose of purifying "the class ranks on the scientific research front," a task that they sought to accomplish by promoting "mass study, criticism, and repudiation" and by "ferreting out" "renegades, enemy agents, capitalist-roaders, and other class enemies" in research units.

One feature of these groups was a distinct distrust of and antagonism toward "intellectuals," as is evident from the following statement made by a representative of one of these thought propaganda teams at

[9] Ibid.

[10] Ibid., 16 September 1967.

[11] NCNA International Service, 21 December 1969, Peking.

a rally, with an estimated attendance of over 2,000 persons, at Shanghai on 9 December 1968:

> Scientific research institutes are places where intellectuals work in concentrated groups. The enemy's presence is evident in these units, and struggle is very complicated. Scientific research units in the main did not take part or took very little part in the political movements after the liberation. For this reason, the tasks in the struggle against the enemy in the scientific research institutes are particularly difficult. . . . We must overcome rightist-inclined lethargy and make a full estimation of the enemy's position. We must grasp the work of purifying the class ranks in the scientific research field and dig out all class enemies hidden in these units. This is a tough fight. It is imperative to keep a firm hold and carry it through thoroughly.[12]

What was reported to have occurred in the Microbiology Institute can perhaps serve as a case study. The Microbiology Institute was typical of most of the leading institutes of the Chinese Academy of Sciences in that the leading scientific personnel of the institute at the time had received their training abroad.[13] It should come as no surprise, then, that the following charges were made against them:

> The majority of the research personnel in this institute are from capitalist families and received bourgeois educations. Even after liberation, their world outlook was not sufficiently remolded because they were influenced by the counterrevolutionary revisionism pushed by the arch renegade Liu Shao-ch'i in the field of scientific research.[14]

They were also accused of having a "bourgeois world outlook and academic viewpoint." In the face of this, the PLA-Mao Tse-tung worker thought propaganda team stationed in the institute, together with their "comrades in the revolutionary committee," concluded that it would be necessary, after a study of Mao's remarks on "proletarian

---

[12] Shanghai City Service, 9 December 1968.
[13] Tai Fang-lan, the director, received his B.S. from Cornell University in 1918 and his M.S. from the University of Michigan; the vice-director, Ch'en Hua-kuei, obtained his Ph.D. from London University in 1939. See Chu-yuan Cheng, *Scientific and Engineering Manpower in Communist China, 1949–1963* (Washington, D.C.: National Science Foundation, 1965), p. 392. Other major staff members included Chou Chia-chih, a research fellow at Cambridge University in 1946–48, Hsiang Wang-nien, Ph.D., Washington University, 1953, Lin Ch'uan-kuang, Ph.D., Cornell University, 1940, and Teng Shu-ch'ün, Ph.D., Cornell University, 1927. See *Selected Scientific Institutions in Mainland China,* ed. Ralph W. Watkins (Stanford: Hoover Institution Press, 1971), pp. 86–87.
[14] Peking Domestic Service, 19 February 1969.

policies concerning intellectuals," to "criticize and repudiate the bourgeois world outlook and academic viewpoint of these research personnel."

In order to achieve this end, the propaganda team assisted the Revolutionary Committee in running a Mao Tse-tung's thought study class. In the first lesson, on "class education," the "research personnel heard reports by veteran workers on the sufferings of the old society as opposed to the happiness of the new society." The scientists also "visited factories and performed manual labor" and through this process "learned the revolutionary spirit and selfless working style of the working class." The report concluded that this effort had been successful and that as a result of the study class

> the scientific research personnel in the Microbiology Institute of the Chinese Academy of Sciences have now taken on a brand new appearance. Some of them have expressed the desire to be criticized and repudiated by the masses so they can transform themselves. Others have asked to be sent to the countryside where they can receive reeducation by the poor and lower-middle peasants.[15]

Similar activities, often of not so gentle a nature, went on at other institutes. "Purification of the class ranks" was carried out by the Mao Tse-tung worker thought propaganda team at the Animal Husbandry Institute of the Chinese Academy of Agricultural Sciences in Lanchow, where the team was reported as being successful in "ferreting out" the "handful" of class enemies at the institute and in "isolating and exposing the handful of obstinate class enemies."[16] Another worker propaganda team entered the Ocean and Aquatic Products Research Institute in Tsingtao to set up Mao Tse-tung's thought study classes. It was said that at a "recent meeting, the revolutionary masses struggled against and dragged out a handful of agents of China's Krushchev, reactionary academic 'authorities,' and other class enemies."[17]

As might be expected, the efforts of the worker propaganda teams on occasion met with resistance, and there are reports of "sabotage" by "capitalist-roaders and class enemies" at various branches of the Chinese Academy of Sciences in southern China. One such recalcitrant group was found at the South Sea Oceanic Research Institute,

---

[15] Ibid.
[16] NCNA Domestic Service, 4 February 1969.
[17] Tsingtao City Service, 12 October 1968.

where some scientific personnel were said to have hindered the "struggle-criticism-transformation campaign" in their units. These individuals did not fare so well, for the majority of the "scientific and technological research personnel" in these units were sent to rural areas to "receive reeducation from the poor and lower-middle peasants."[18]

In short, this period was one of great disruption of activity at research institutes throughout the nation while research workers were subjected to reeducation and on occasion discipline for the ultimate purpose of redirecting their activities toward state-specified goals. Gradually this period of attack against the sciences and the scientists appears to have given way to the redirection of research and the reconstitution of the institutes along new lines.

Reconstitution of Scientific Research

Once the research workers of an institute had undergone reeducation, the next step appears to have been their "integration" with the workers and peasants. Scientists were strongly encouraged, if not forced, to leave their laboratories and work closely with workers and farmers.

The scientific workers of the Institute of Genetics, for example, as a result of their repudiation of the revisionist line in scientific research during the Cultural Revolution, "came to see that scientific research must serve the socialist revolution and socialist construction and the workers, peasants and soldiers."[19] One of the research problems with which they were confronted was that of developing a "high sugar content pig feed that would serve the cause of building socialism," a task requiring the breeding of the fungus *Aspergillus niger* with which corncobs or stalks of maize could be fermented. Not having succeeded in doing this in their "well-equipped laboratories," they turned to the poor and lower-middle peasants for suggestions. The latter, "displaying revolutionary initiative," developed methods for maintaining stable temperatures, humidity, and ventilation of the fermenting feed under primitive conditions, with the result that sufficient fungus was produced to "ferment feed for 500 pigs." Hailing this achievement, the poor and lower-middle peasants, in a statement that surely was not lost on the nation's scientists, were reported to have said,

---

[18] Ibid.
[19] NCNA International Service, 16 January 1969, Peking.

18

the scientists and technicians, in leaving their laboratories and carrying out scientific experiments with us, are acting in line with our great leader Chairman Mao's teachings. Their action conforms to our hope, and the road they have taken is a right one.[20]

Another interesting story involves scientists of the Institute of Botany who were approached by members of a commune with a request to help them cure a form of cabbage rot. The matter was pushed aside because the botanists felt that treating cabbage rot was not their job and would be a waste of time. To the members of the PLA-Mao Tsetung worker thought propaganda team, however, this was a matter of importance. In their eyes, the botanists' decision to drop the study on cabbage rot, involving as it did the question of whom scientific research should serve, reflected the influence of the revisionist line in research. Consequently, the scientific and research workers, "led by the propaganda team and the Revolutionary Committee, organized a work team" to attend to the problem. They were joined by personnel from the Vegetable Research Institute and the Zoology Institute. We are told that the scientists then succeeded in developing methods for preventing and treating the cabbage rot.[21]

Scientists were encouraged to learn from the peasants and to benefit from their "abundant experience." Staff members of institutes were sent in alternating groups to the countryside and we have reports of how the down-to-earth knowledge of the peasants has assisted scientists in solving problems. Scientists from the Entomology Institute, for example, were said to have been assisted in breeding a chalcid fly, the eggs of which are parasitic to paddy borers in rice-growing areas of Hainan:

> Based on scientific data, they knew that the chalcid fly lived as a parasite only on the white tip sugarcane borer and the paddy borer. But peasants told them that such flies could also live on the egg masses of the brown paddy borer. With clues offered by the peasants, they made a survey of the eggs of twenty-six different kinds of insects and verified that both the brown paddy borer and the sugarcane borer could be used as substitute hosts.[22]

The next step beyond benefiting from the knowledge of the peasants is to base decisions on what research projects will be undertaken

---

[20] Ibid.
[21] Ibid., 21 December 1969, Peking.
[22] Ibid., 10 February 1974, Peking.

19

on the peasants' needs in the field.   While this is standard practice at experimental agricultural stations throughout the world, we have indisputable evidence that in China even some of the research projects of the Genetics Institute have been determined by local needs.   In the case in question, scientists from the Genetics Institute had been sent to the countryside to become integrated with the peasants.   While working with the peasants, they found that the peasants "were in need of a new breeding method to prevent the separation of offspring of hybrid strains and shorten the breeding period."   As a result, the scientists started research on pollen culture in April 1970 and after two years of effort succeeded in "obtaining rice and wheat plants by pollen culture."   They were also reported to have engaged in studies that resulted in "shortening the time needed for breeding."[23]   In this instance we have confirmation that the story is not apocryphal from the published literature, including several studies on this topic by researchers at the Genetics Institute.[24]   In addition, "joint scientific experiments by members of the Genetics Institute of the Chinese Academy of Sciences and workers and peasants" were credited with improving crop strains and preventing potato degeneration.[25]

In agricultural science itself, there was criticism of scientists in well-equipped agricultural scientific research institutes who had accomplished little because they had followed the counterrevolutionary revisionist line on agricultural science.   One proposed remedy was to put leadership in agricultural science in the hands of the working class and of the poor and lower-middle peasants.

> The situation wherein bourgeois intellectuals influence agricultural scientific research must be thoroughly changed. Chairman Mao's proletarian line on scientific research must prevail.   We must set up scientific research stations at rural communes so that scientific research will directly serve socialist agricultural production.   Scientific research personnel must go to the front line of agricultural production and integrate themselves with the poor and lower-middle peas-

---

[23] Ibid., 2 April 1973, Peking.

[24] See, for example, "Induction of Plants with Pollen from *in vitro* Cultivation of Wheat Anthers," *Genetics Bulletin*, no. 2 (1973), "Factors for the Induction *in vitro* of Plantelets from Pollen Grains and Research in the Genetics of Plantelets of Rice," *Genetics Bulletin*, no. 2 (1973), and "Investigation of the Induction and Genetic Expression of Rice Pollen Plants," *Scientia Sinica*, vol. 17, no. 2 (1974).   These studies were the products of the Third Laboratory of the Institute of Genetics.

[25] NCNA, 9 April 1973, Peking.

ants, receive reeducation by the latter, and conduct scientific experiments for the development of agricultural production.[26]

By the 1970s we begin to get reports of scientists from agricultural research institutes going out into rural areas and conducting experiments in conjunction with peasants. Thus we are told that the "scientific research personnel" of the Nenchiang Region Agricultural Science Research Institute in Heilungkiang Province had worked in rural production brigades, "eating, living and working together with the supporting masses and conducting scientific experiments together with them." It was reported that the institute, working together with the Nenchiang Regional Bureau of Science and Technology, had undertaken a program of "agricultural technical cooperation among peasants" and that over the past few years they had completed "more than 130 coordinated farming and research projects."[27]

In southern China, the "scientific research personnel" of the Kweichow Provincial Academy of Agricultural Sciences did much the same thing. However, they also "helped local communes and brigades run short-term training classes and have trained more than 300 agricultural technicians," a service that "created favorable conditions for the development of mass scientific experimentation."[28] Similarly, roughly 400 members of the Shensi Branch of the Chinese Academy of Agricultural Sciences were reported to have conducted experiments on 430 topics in 100 production brigades in that province.[29]

One of the most interesting features of this whole movement to the countryside was the development of "mass scientific experimentation," a concept first formulated during the Great Leap Forward of 1958, but which in the 1970s appears to have been a direct outgrowth of the "integration" of agricultural scientists with farmers in the fields.[30] As Table 1 shows, in this form of experimentation scientists or technicians often took the leading role, directing commune members

[26] Fukien Provincial Service, 31 January 1969, Foochow.
[27] Heilungkiang Provincial Service, 18 March 1972, Harbin.
[28] NCNA Domestic Service, 19 March 1972, Peking.
[29] NCNA International Service, 28 June 1972, Peking.
[30] It was at the time of the Great Leap Forward that the idea of demystification of the sciences was put forward, with the assertion that scientific research was something that could be done by the masses at the local level and that it need not be confined to specialists in expensively equipped laboratories. This view of science as a potential mass activity was clearly enunciated in an editorial in the *People's Daily* of 18 June 1958. See *Ch'ün-chung K'o-hsüeh Yen-chiu Wen-chi* (Peking: K'o-hsüeh P'u-chi Ch'u-pan-she, 1958), vol. 1, pp. 1–2.

Table 1
REPRESENTATIVE MASS EXPERIMENTS REPORTED IN 1973–74

Place, Date	Personnel	Project
Kwangtung Province, 1972	Members of communes; scientists and agrotechnicians	Development of new strain of typhoon-resistant rice, measures against rice borers and pests, hybrid maize and sorghum strains
Nationwide, 1971–72	Thirty-three scientific and technical service groups of the Chinese Academy of Agricultural Sciences	Cultivation of superior varieties of crops, experiments on farming techniques, soils, and fertilizers, plant diseases and insect pests, afforestation, livestock improvement and disease control
Yunnan Province, 1971–72	47,000 scientific research groups made up of 180,000 commune and brigade cadres, poor and lower-middle peasants, and agrotechnicians	Development of fine-strain rice, wheat, cotton, and rape seeds, studies of plant disease and insect control, chemical fertilizers, and agricultural chemicals
Shansi Province, since Cultural Revolution	Staff of Luliang Region Agricultural Science Research Institute and 850 commune members admitted to the institute to study technical data and conduct scientific experiments	Cultivation of forty-two fine strains of wheat, sorghum, cotton, corn and millet; exchange of ideas, techniques, and experiences with more than 100 commune farms and brigade scientific research groups
Anhwei Province, 1971–72	About 400,000 people, largely low and lower-middle peasants	Development of fifty new strains of grains, cotton, and oil-producing crops; spread use of new wheat strains; soil improvement; logical control of plant diseases and insect pests
Nationwide, 1972	Guiding personnel from the Chinese Academy of Agricultural and Forestry Services and more than 100 scientific research and production units	Mass testing of new insecticides and evaluation of their effects

Source: In order of table entries: NCNA, 17 February 1973, Peking; NCNA Domestic Service, 17 March 1973, Peking; Yunnan Provincial Service, 24 March 1973, Kunming; NCNA Domestic Service, 4 August 1973, Peking; Anhwei Provincial Service, 30 September 1973, Hofei; NCNA Domestic Service, 11 October 1973, Peking.

in carrying out what might be described as data-intensive testing. This type of mass experimentation was characteristic of the early 1970s and was consistent with what appears to be a general policy of relying on mass participation in areas, such as weather prediction, in which large amounts of data are necessary. It marks a significant departure from traditional approaches to scientific study.

The effort in meteorology shows that the mass approach has not been limited to agricultural science. The Chinese report that the countryside of China is "studded with about 10,000 meteorological posts, numerous weather observation posts, and rain-measuring stations." The main function of these is, of course, to serve agricultural production. It is reported that they are "integrated with local experimental groups"[31] and that they supply meteorological information to higher-level weather stations.[32]

It should be noted in passing that education in the sciences has also been affected by the call to integrate with the masses, with many institutions reporting the establishment of the so-called three-in-one system, in which teaching, production, and scientific experimentation are linked. One example of the linking of academic institutions with production is that of the Changchun Geological Institute, from which, beginning in 1974, more than "two thousand teachers, students, staff members and workers" went out to "thirty-one plants, mines and geological teams in Kirin, Liaoning, Shantung, Hopei, Honan, Shensi, Inner Mongolia and Kiangsi" provinces as well as to other areas. An example of their activities follows:

> The teachers and students of the first-year class of the Instruments Department linked with the Changchun Municipal Geological Instruments Repair and Manufacturing Plant. They turned the plant's workshops into classrooms. By fulfilling production tasks, the workers of the plant taught the students both basic and vocational knowledge regarding geological instruments as well as technical lessons. They also learned how to handle all instruments and meters, and mastered welding techniques.[33]

A few additional examples of this sort of activity should suffice:

---

[31] "Meteorological Posts in the Countryside," *Peking Review,* no. 49 (6 December 1974), p. 23.
[32] NCNA, 20 October 1974, Peking.
[33] Kirin Provincial Service, 7 October 1974, Changchun.

23

In engaging in the three great revolutionary movements, some of the institute teachers and students went to the Chaoyang Region, Liaoning, to solve the question of water sources in the movement to learn from Tachai in agriculture. Some teachers and students took part in the campaign to locate diamond deposits in order to solve the state's urgent needs. Others devoted their efforts to finding phosphorus deposits for agricultural production.[34]

In addition to reports like these, the organizations with which contributors to the scientific journals are associated corroborate the fact that research work has become more closely linked with agricultural and industrial production. For example, the authors of a paper on the elimination of locust infestations in a particular lake district were associated with the Bureau of Agriculture of the Chi-ning District Revolutionary Committee (Shantung Province) and with the Laboratory of Insect Ecology of the Institute of Zoology.[35] A study on biological control of the corn borer was a joint project of the Institute of Plant Protection, the Kirin Province Academy of Agricultural Science, and the Experimental Agricultural Science Station of the Ts'ai Chia People's Commune.[36] Similarly, a study of damage to winter wheat was reported as a joint venture by the Three-in-One Combination Experimental Group of the East-is-Red Brigade of the Hsin-tien People's Commune (Shensi), the Agricultural Technique Popularization Station of the Yu-lin District (Shensi), the Agricultural Work Station of Sui-te Hsien, and the Sixth Laboratory of the Institute of Botany (CAS).[37]

Universities, too, have become involved in collaborative efforts. A study of the production of acids by fermentation of n-alkanes was done by the Research Group of Petroleum Fermentation of the Shing-Shen Fermentation Factory and members of the Department of Biology of Futan University, one of China's leading universities.[38] Among groups that may be operating on a continuing basis is the Luminous Fungus Cooperative Research Group of Kiangsu Province, made up of the Department of Biology of Nanking University, the Department of Forestry of the Nanking Engineering Institute, the Kiangsu College of New Medicine, the Nanking Institute of Materia Medica, and the

---

[34] Ibid.
[35] See *Acta Entomologica Sinica*, vol. 17, no. 3 (1974).
[36] Ibid., vol. 16, no. 2 (1974).
[37] See *Acta Botanica Sinica*, vol. 16, no. 2 (1974).
[38] See *Acta Microbiologica Sinica*, vol. 13, no. 1 (1973).

Chen-Chiang Pharmaceutical Factory.[39] Collaborative efforts involving major academic or research institutes and local factories and organizations appear to be more common in the biological and agricultural sciences than in the physical sciences.

Thus, in the process of redirecting the course of the sciences, China's political leaders have attempted to bring the scientists into closer contact with the working classes. Conversely, it has been their policy to effect the popularization of the sciences throughout the society. With little doubt, the programs of mass experimentation have contributed to a greater awareness of scientific ways of attacking problems among those peasants who have taken part in them. For the literate, there are such popular periodicals dealing with the sciences as *Fossils* (*Hua-shih*), *Radio* (*Wu-Hsien-tien*), *Geographical Knowledge* (*Ti-li Chih-shih*), and *Scientific Experiment* (*Ke Xue Shi Yan*), which are monthly publications. *Scientific Experiment* deals with a wide range of topics, from natural pest control, the mechanism of acupuncture, and Chinese herbal medicines to electrical circuits, meteorology, and marine life.

In addition to periodicals, a large number of books on the sciences are published by the Science Publishing House and other organs. These books are meant to "serve the workers, peasants and soldiers as well as industrial and agricultural production."[40] In the first quarter of 1973 the Science Publishing House was reported to have issued a total of thirty-three books on science and technology and to be planning to publish fifty books in the second quarter of the year. These included such titles as *Hybrid Kaoliang, Evolution of Life, Economical Cross-Breeding of Hogs,* and *Liquid Fertilizer.*[41] Other publishing ventures planned for 1973 were a series of textbooks for the technical education of workers to be put out by the Machinery Industry Publishing House, and a series of booklets on the natural sciences covering more than thirty subjects for the purpose of popularizing the natural sciences among the "broad masses of workers, peasants, soldiers and youngsters," to be issued by the People's Publishing House in Peking.

Another field in which there has been active publication is medicine and health, the People's Health Publishing House having put out seventy-four books over the 1971–72 period, including *Teaching Mate-*

[39] Ibid., vol. 14, no. 1 (1974).
[40] NCNA Domestic Service, 25 April 1973, Peking.
[41] Ibid. (no Chinese titles given).

rials for Barefoot Doctors, Eye Care, and *Discussions on Common Sense Hygiene for Women in Rural Areas.*[42] For young people, the Shanghai People's Publishing House in 1973–74 developed a series called "Self-Study Collection for Young People." Two of the texts available outside China dealt with hygiene and human physiology and were amply illustrated and written in clear, simple style.

The importance attached to the popularization of the sciences is evident from the fact that the party journal *Red Flag (Hung Ch'i)* printed a long review of a revised edition of a set of books entitled *One-Hundred-Thousand Why's (Shi Wan Ge Weishenme)* issued by the People's Publishing House.[43] The series was originally published in 1962 and the first revised version appeared in 1965. The set consists of twelve volumes averaging about 240 pages each and is made up of short sections covering topics ranging over the fields of mathematics, physics, chemistry, astronomy, meteorology, geography, biology, medicine, and engineering technology. Most are written in a simple, direct style and draw on concrete experience, although some deal with relatively difficult mathematical formulations.

From the foregoing discussion, we can see that the years since 1966 have been eventful ones for the sciences in China, marked by the intensification of political control of scientific research and the rise of a utilitarian view of scientific research. Perhaps the main concerns and trends in science policy in China can best be summed up by the six tasks that the delegates to a scientific and technological conference in Kiangsi Province set out for themselves in March 1973:

> (1) It is necessary to continue to grasp firmly and well the task of prime importance—criticism of revisionism and rectification of the style of work, to study assiduously works by Marx, Lenin, and Chairman Mao, and to enhance one's ability to distinguish between genuine and sham Marxism. It is necessary to penetratingly criticize the revolutionary fallacies and counterrevolutionary crimes of swindlers like Liu Shao-ch'i for promoting idealist apriorism and sabotaging the party's policy toward intellectuals, and to eliminate completely their remnant pernicious influence by grasping the essence of their counterrevolutionary revisionist line and by linking criticism

---

[42] Ibid., 3 May 1973 (no Chinese titles given).
[43] Ti Ch'ing, "Reading Materials for the Popularization of Science Should Vividly Propagate Dialectical Materialism," *Hung Ch'i,* no. 11 (November 1973), pp. 68–72.

26

with reality in the struggle between the two lines on the scientific-technological front in our province.

(2) It is necessary to further promote the concept of taking agriculture as the foundation, continue on with agro-scientific research projects, grasp well research projects connected with industry supporting agriculture, and do a good job in research work on agricultural machinery with the objective of promoting agricultural mechanization in our province and contributing to the work involved in having our province surpass the grain production quota set in the national program for agricultural development.

(3) It is necessary to further implement in an all-round manner the party's policy of uniting with, educating and re-forming intellectuals, fully arouse the socialist enthusiasm of scientific-technological personnel and, at the same time, go all out to train scientific-technological personnel from among the workers, peasants and soldiers in order to build up a mighty contingent of scientific-technological workers.

(4) It is necessary to continue to deepen the mass movement on scientific experiments and to integrate this with specialized scientific research to make the two complement and promote each other.

(5) It is necessary to step up investigation and study, conscientiously carry out in the current year essential scientific research projects for the province, formulate scientific-technological development plans for the whole province for the period 1973–1980, strengthen scientific-technological research work and do a good job in controlling and standardizing weights and measurements.

(6) It is necessary to further strengthen the party's leadership over scientific-technological work and resolutely carry out the struggle-criticism-transformation tasks in the scientific-technological field. Party committees at all levels must place scientific-technological work on their agenda as an important task, grasp it firmly and well, put specific personnel in charge of it, and strengthen scientific-technological management work at the provincial, regional, municipal, and county levels.[44]

---

[44] Kiangsi Provincial Service, 15 March 1973, Nanchang. The conference was attended by 420 persons from "scientific and technological units at the provincial, regional, municipal and county levels, responsible persons of scientific-technological groups, scientific research departments in universities, colleges and institutes, and factories, mines and hospitals run by the province, as well as scientific-technological cadres." From March to June 1973 there were at least four other similar provincial level conferences whose primary objectives apparently were to maintain the indoctrination of scientific workers and set forth state policies toward the sciences.

The ideal, then, is a community of scientists working under a planned program of carefully allocated human and material resources to achieve those goals most necessary for the society as a whole, a community devoted not to personal fame and self-aggrandizement, not to science as something of intrinsic value, not to the internal logic of any given scientific discipline, but to the needs of China and its citizens and to the services that the scientific disciplines can render in bettering the lives of the people, building the economy, and strengthening the international position of China.

While it is possible for this idea to prevail, to all outward appearances, because of the sheer power inherent in the political sector of Chinese society, it must not be assumed that it has not met with resistance and that considerable backsliding has not and will not occur. This can be inferred from the vigor, at times the ferocity, of the attacks against the scientists at the leading institutes during the Cultural Revolution.   There is an inevitable tension between the political sector and the scientific community, which may well lead to further attacks against the latter and therefore to further disruptions of the course of scientific research.   Since policies toward education and scientific research are closely linked to the power struggle between the "moderate" and ultra-leftist factions that erupted following the death of Premier Chou En-lai, a clearer picture of the extent of dissension over science policy between the political and scientific sectors and within the scientific sector may emerge with time.

2
The State of Scientific Research after the Cultural Revolution

Given the utilitarian view of science propounded during the Cultural Revolution, we should expect the scientific research currently being pursued in China to be concerned with practical and applied studies. We could also expect to find that whatever programs of basic research existed up to 1966 had been largely abandoned. In this chapter, we shall test the rhetoric of the Cultural Revolution against China's current record in the sciences.

In attempting to assess the overall state of scientific research in China we are faced with a major obstacle in that China is not yet fully open to us. For information we are dependent on what visitors, who are usually taken to the major institutes, can pick up and on what the Chinese themselves tell us either in press and radio statements, often laced with propaganda, or in the literature published in scientific journals. Unfortunately, visitors remain for only brief periods of time and are not necessarily able to make repeat visits. Moreover, those who do not speak Chinese must rely on interpreters whose functions undoubtedly include checking on the sort of information that is passed. On the other hand, Chinese radio and press releases tend to emphasize achievements, rather than to present a balanced assessment of what is actually going on. Caution must also be used in assessing domestic radio and press statements, from which we obtain most of our information about mass experimentation and other local scientific activity, since their actual purpose may well be domestic propaganda.

We are left then with only one consistent and concrete source of information: the published literature. There are serious methodological difficulties in taking the literature as a basis of analysis. Published papers can at best represent only a fraction of the total amount of work being pursued in any given discipline, and, because of the time lag between the completion of a piece of research and the publication of a written account of it, journal articles are apt to be more indicative of work that has been completed than of current research. Nevertheless, the published literature furnishes many valuable clues: the relative amounts of published work in various fields, the degree of specialization of journals, and the institutions in which research is being conducted. The relative volume of publication and the degree of journal specialization are strong indications of the fields that are being emphasized, while the subject matter of the papers selected for publication may further reflect national priorities as well as the quality and general sophistication of research. The locations and types of institutions with which authors are affiliated provide an overall picture of the extent of centralization or decentralization in research programs.

The picture that emerges is merely the tip of the iceberg. Nevertheless, the visible, published research must surely stand in significant relation to the total volume of research in respect to the relative priority placed upon the disciplines. From a statistical standpoint, certainly, it represents far more than a mere random sample. With this caveat for preface, let us take a close look at the scientific literature published since the Cultural Revolution through 1974.

Scientific Literature, 1966–74

The most striking contrast between the period up to 1966 and the period considered here is the distinct and considerable decrease in the total volume of publication, reflected primarily in the number of journals appearing. Table 2 shows the decline in the number of major journals being published. In addition to the journals noted in the table, six major college or university scientific journals have not reappeared. In the field of agricultural research, not only *Chinese Agricultural Sciences,* the organ of the Chinese Academy of Agricultural Sciences, but also seven major regional agricultural college journals have failed to reappear. In the field of engineering, there has been no sign of nine journals published before the Cultural Revolution by various engineering societies or colleges.

In medicine, there were before the Cultural Revolution, in addition to the *Chinese Medical Journal* (*Chung-hua I-hsüeh Tsa-chih*), ten major specialized journals as well as at least ten leading journals

Table 2

MAJOR SCIENTIFIC JOURNALS PUBLISHED BEFORE AND AFTER THE CULTURAL REVOLUTION

(excluding medicine)

Journals Published until 1966; Publication Not Resumed		Journals Published until 1966; Publication Resumed after 1972	Journals Inaugurated since 1972
Acta Zootaxonomica Sinica	Oceanologica et Limnologica Sinica	Acta Zoologica Sinica	Scientia Geologica Sinica
Acta Horticulturalia Sinica	Acta Electronica Sinica	Acta Botanica Sinica	Geochimica
Acta Biologiae Experimentalis Sinica	Acta Automatica Sinica	Acta Phytotaxonomica Sinica	Physics
Acta Pharmaceutica Sinica	Acta Mechanica Sinica	Acta Entomologica Sinica	Chemistry Bulletin
Acta Physiologica Sinica	Acta Chimica Sinica	Acta Microbiologica Sinica	Acta Genetica Sinica
Acta Anatomica Sinica	Polymer Communications	Acta Geophysica Sinica	Genetics Bulletin
Acta Nutrimenta Sinica	Acta Veterinaria et Zootechnica	Acta Geologica Sinica	Application and Knowledge of Mathematics
Acta Paleontologica Sinica	Scientiae Silvae	Vertebrata Palasiatica	Journal of Tsing Hua University and Peking University on Science and Technology
Acta Pedologica Sinica	Acta Phytopathologica Sinica	Acta Physica Sinica	
Acta Meteorologica Sinica		Acta Mathematica Sinica	
Acta Geodetica et Limnologica Sinica		Acta Astronomica Sinica	
		Scientia Sinica	
		Science Bulletin	

Number of major scientific journals published before the Cultural Revolution: 33
Number of major scientific journals published since the Cultural Revolution: 21

Source: Author's compilation.

31

published by medical colleges. Today, only the *Chinese Medical Journal* remains. In its present form this journal usually publishes in a single issue only about half the number of articles it formerly ran. As a result, publication in the medical field may be at about one-twentieth of its pre-Cultural Revolution volume. One other major casualty of the Cultural Revolution has been the *Acta Psychologica Sinica*, which reflects the unhappy state of psychology in recent years. The Chinese Psychological Association was abolished during the Cultural Revolution and psychology was dropped from the university curriculum.[1]

It is clear, then, that scientific publication has not yet returned to its former volume. This may be simply a reflection of the disruptions of research caused by the Cultural Revolution or it may be a signal of a change, a decrease in the amount of research being conducted or a new reluctance on the part of Chinese scientists to put their work into print until they are certain of their results. One could argue from the latter standpoint that the campaign to make science a vehicle for serving the people rather than a means for acquiring "fame and fortune" may play a part in diminishing the level of publication. On the other hand, the diversion of scientists to factories and the countryside to solve practical problems must certainly have taken time away from the sort of research that would result in papers in serious journals.

One plausible explanation is that there simply is not a sufficient number of scholarly papers to support a larger number of journals. This possibility is consistent with the finding that a fair number of papers published in 1973 and 1974 were based on data or specimens obtained before the Cultural Revolution, often as early as 1961 and in one case as far back as 1958. These included two papers in the *Acta Botanica Sinica*, four papers in the *Acta Zoologica Sinica*, eight papers in the *Acta Entomologica Sinica*, two papers in the *Acta Microbiologica Sinica*, and three papers in *Vertebrata Palaseatica*. While this may represent a process of catching up on publication, it may also indicate that research workers in some areas have fallen behind in their work or have not yet had time to carry out new projects.

The types of journals now being published in China also furnish valuable clues about the reorientation of priorities that has taken place and about the general levels of development of the various scientific disciplines. We shall return to the topic of shifts in research emphasis

---

[1] Albert H. Yee, "Psychology in China Bows to the Cultural Revolution," *APA Monitor*, vol. 4, no. 3 (March 1973), pp. 1 and 4.

in greater detail later, but it should be pointed out here that, while there is a preponderance of journals in the biological and geological sciences reflecting the importance placed upon these disciplines, among the journals no longer published are several that dealt almost exclusively with basic biological and medical research. As we shall see, it is in this area that major shifts in priorities have occurred.

By far the most important clue to the overall state of development of the sciences in China is the generally unspecialized character of the professional journals. In the biological sciences, to be sure, separate journals are issued for the major subdisciplines. We do not find, however, the further breakdown so common in Western journals—journals of medical entomology, insect physiology, experimental zoology, virology, molecular biology, membrane biology, or cytology, for example. The field of chemistry is represented solely by *Chemistry Bulletin* (*Hua-hsüeh T'ung-pao*); there are no journals of organic, inorganic, physical, or polymer chemistry, to name only a few of the categories more common in the West. Of considerable interest is the fact that journal specialization in biological and medical research has decreased since 1966, while that in the geological sciences has increased.

This clearly suggests that the research efforts being made in the major disciplines are not sufficiently large to support or justify extensive journal specialization. If journal specialization is any index of the degree of scientific development, scientific research remains at a far lower level in China than in the United States, Japan, or the Soviet Union.

Further appreciation of the relative priority given to the various fields of science can be obtained from the numbers of papers published in the various specialized branches. Table 3 shows a breakdown of published papers by field. The preponderance of papers in the biological and earth sciences is a direct reflection of journal specialization in these fields and without doubt an indirect reflection of the relative proportions of research going on in these fields and other disciplines. This is to be expected in a nation in which the development of health care, agriculture, and natural resources is a prerequisite to eventual industrialization and emergence as a major world power. Nevertheless, the proportional distribution of papers among fields is not necessarily indicative of relative budgetary investment in that a good deal of the research done in the biological sciences can be carried out rather inexpensively by individual scientists while much of that in physics requires expensive equipment and teams of scientists.

Table 3

OUTPUT OF PAPERS SINCE RESUMPTION OF PUBLICATION,
1972 TO JULY 1974

(excluding medicine)

	Published Papers	
Field	Number	Percentage
Biological sciences		
Zoology and entomology	145	21.1
Botany	100	14.6
Microbiology	57	8.3
Genetics	29	4.2
Subtotal	331	48.3
Earth sciences		
Geology	86	12.5
Palaeontology	64	9.3
Meteorology	11	1.6
Subtotal	161	23.4
Physics	64	9.3
Mathematics	54	7.9
Chemistry	48	7.0
Astronomy	28	4.1
Total	686	100.0

Source: Author's survey of major scientific journals.

These same proportions hold generally true when we look at the numbers of papers contributed by given institutions. Table 4 shows the numbers of papers contributed by what, from the standpoint of their volume of publication, appear to be the most active centers of research. It should be noted that these figures refer specifically to the number of papers published in affiliation with an institution and not to the number of writers. They do not include papers for which the affiliations of the authors were not listed. (Sixty of the papers surveyed in the field of geology, for instance, did not identify the affiliations of the authors.) Thus, these figures should be viewed as presenting a general and far from complete picture.

In any event, it is clear that research is concentrated in a relatively small number of institutes and academic institutions: as Table 5 shows,

94 percent of the papers originating from research institutes were produced by 7 percent of the institutes contributing papers, and 90.3 percent of the papers originating from academic institutions were produced by 14.5 percent of these. Nevertheless, while large-scale research programs are under way at major institutes and universities and the studies emerging from the major institutes centered about Peking are preponderant, there is some degree of decentralization of effort throughout the nation. As indicated previously, one interesting feature of this diversification is that a fair number of papers are contributed by staff members of industrial plants and even by members of commune research teams. It is also worth noting that the research institutes have contributed considerably more papers than the colleges and universities.

Of equal interest are those institutes active before the Cultural Revolution that contributed only one paper each during the period of the survey. These include the Institute of Pharmacology, the Institute of Experimental Biology, the Institute of Meteorology, the Institute of Biophysics, the Institute of Geography, and the Institute of Geochemistry. (It is possible that the Institute of Geochemistry does not belong on this list in the light of the numerous studies in the field of geology for which author affiliations were not provided.) What significance this may have will be discussed under the summaries of research in the various disciplines.

The picture in medical research in 1973 seems to have been generally similar, with affiliates of the Chinese Academy of Medical Sciences contributing 28 (about 36 percent) out of the 77 papers whose authors were identified as to institutional affiliation. These 77 papers, however, were only about a third of the 245 papers published in the *Chinese Medical Journal* in 1973. Thus, we do not have sufficient information on which to base an assessment of the relative importance of the centers of medical research now active in China.

Of more interest to persons contemplating cooperative studies or exchanges with Chinese scientific research institutions is the actual content of research. While limitations of space do not permit a detailed account of research in the various disciplines, we will attempt to present general summaries by field in the sections that follow.

The Biological Sciences. For the sake of convenience, we will discuss developments in the biological sciences under the headings of zoology, entomology, botany, genetics, and microbiology, divisions that corre-

Table 4

CENTERS OF SCIENTIFIC RESEARCH MOST ACTIVE SINCE THE CULTURAL REVOLUTION

(excluding medicine)

Institution	Papers Published since 1972	Institution	Papers Published since 1972
Research institutes		Institute of Materia Medica	4
Institute of Vertebrate Paleontology and Paleoanthropology	49	Institute of Biochemistry	4
Institute of Zoology	48	Institute of Geology	4
Institute of Botany	33	Institute of Atmospheric Physics	4
Institute of Microbiology	20	Peking Zoo[a]	4
Institute of Physics	17	Colleges and universities	
Institute of Mathematics	15	Peking University	19
Atomic Energy Institute	12	Nankai University	12
Institute of Geophysics	10	Futan University	12
Institute of Genetics	8	Kuangtung College of Agriculture and Forestry	10
Peking Observatory	7	Peking Normal University	6
Institute of Chemistry	6	Amoy University	6
Yunnan Zoological Research Institute	6	Nanking University	6
Institute of Epidemiology	5	Lanchow University	6
Institute of Entomology	5	Kirin University	5
Kirin Institute of Applied Chemistry	5	Northwestern University	4
Szechuan Biological Research Institute	5	Chung Shan University	4
Institute of Plant Physiology	5	Kueiyang Medical College	4
Nanking Institute of Geology and Paleontology	5		

[a] The contribution of the Peking Zoo may be an anomaly in that the papers dealt solely with the giant panda. Therefore, it is not particularly likely that the Peking Zoo will remain among those institutions with high publication frequencies.

Note: This is a selected list consisting of institutions whose members have written four or more published scientific papers.

Source: Author's survey of major scientific journals.

Table 5

ORIGIN OF PUBLISHED RESEARCH PAPERS, 1972 TO JULY 1974

(excluding medicine)

Institutions		Papers	
Number	Percent of total	Number	Percent of total
Research institutes			
3 most productive	2	130	58
11 most productive	7	210	94
108 contributing one paper each	71	108	48.2
Total institutes contributing papers: 153	100	224	100
Colleges and universities			
4 most productive	5.8	41	66.1
10 most productive	14.5	56	90.3
41 contributing one paper each	60	41	66.1
Total colleges and universities contributing papers: 69	100	62	100

Note: This table is based on a survey by institution of the papers published in the twenty-one major scientific journals appearing since the Cultural Revolution (journals listed in Table 2). All institutions whose members are known to have contributed to published papers are included. Only papers by authors whose institutional affiliations are known are included, and each paper is attributed to each of the institutions with which the author or authors are affiliated. Because of joint authorship and multiple affiliations, the figures for the separate categories of institutions do not add up to the totals for all institutions.

Source: Author's compilation.

spond with those used by the Chinese, even though in actual practice some of these fields are not mutually exclusive.

Zoology. A survey of progress in the zoological sciences during the first ten years of the People's Republic by Cheng Tien-hsi indicated that by 1961 the contribution of Chinese zoologists had been "largely restricted to descriptive or observational reports." The major areas of effort had been "taxonomy, morphology, ecology, and distribution," while experimental biology was still in the "initial stage of development." Cheng concluded that Chinese zoologists had yet to make an original contribution to their science.[2]

---

[2] Cheng Tien-hsi, "Zoological Sciences since 1949," in *Sciences in Communist China,* ed. Sidney H. Gould (Washington, D. C.: American Association for the Advancement of Science, 1961), p. 223.

During the period from 1961 up to the outbreak of the Cultural Revolution in 1966, Chinese zoologists, while continuing the trend of the first decade, undertook further studies in experimental biology and physiology, most of which were published in the now defunct journals *Acta Biologiae Experimentalis Sinica* and *Acta Physiologica Sinica,* with the more traditional zoological studies tending to appear in the *Acta Zoologica Sinica.* In 1965–66, a total of nineteen papers were devoted to experimental zoological studies in the three journals (sixteen of them in the *Acta Biologiae Experimentalis Sinica*), while ten ecological or life-history studies and twenty-six taxonomic or distributional studies appeared, all in the *Acta Zoologica Sinica.* With only the *Acta Zoologica Sinica* resuming publication after the Cultural Revolution, avenues for the publication of zoological studies have been substantially reduced. The current pattern of publication more closely resembles that of the decade up to 1961 than that of the five years immediately preceding the Cultural Revolution.

Thus, of sixty-eight studies reported from January 1972 to July 1974, twenty-six were taxonomic or distributional studies and seven were life histories or environmental studies. There were an additional seventeen studies dealing with human and animal parasites. Most of these were descriptive studies, although there was one study on experimental transmission between human and animal hosts. Physiological, histochemical, and experimental biological studies together accounted for ten of the papers and of the others one paper was on animal pathology, two in the realm of embryology and developmental biology, and one a morphological study. There were also four papers on various aspects of caring for and breeding the giant panda.

Thus it can be said that the more traditional aspects of the discipline have so far dominated the published zoological studies—the discovery and description of new species, the detailing of their life histories, and the discovery and description of parasites. The physiological studies published were also traditional.

Entomology. What holds true for zoology proper also holds true for entomology, with taxonomic studies accounting for a large proportion of the papers, perhaps partly a reflection of the loss of the *Acta Zootaxonomica Sinica,* in which about half of the papers dealt with insect taxonomy. Thus, of seventy-six papers published during the period of the survey, forty-one (54 percent) were taxonomic studies, dealing largely with descriptions of new species. Eleven were studies relating to life histories and economic entomology. Of the seven physiological studies, several were clearly directed toward the practical goal of control of harmful insects. Of considerable interest was the fact that there were eleven studies dealing with biological control of insect pests as against six studies on chemical control. This suggests a change in direction since 1966, when there were eight papers on chemical control as opposed to only two on biological control. One additional journal, *Entomological Knowledge* (*K'un-ch'ung Chih-shih*), which was not surveyed in detail for this paper, is concerned largely with insect pests and means for their control. Available issues of this journal confirm that the preference for biological over chemical control of insect pests is growing.

In general, then, research in zoology and entomology now appears to give less emphasis to physiological and experimental biological studies than during the period immediately preceding the Cultural Revolution, with great stress being laid on taxonomic work and surveys of existing fauna. In entomology in particular, studies tend to be concentrated on groups that are of agricultural and medical importance.

Botany. It was the conclusion of the American scientist Hui-lin Li that botanical research in China during the decade 1951–61 was primarily of an applied nature and that development in the field was uneven.[3] Thus, taxonomy and physiology were felt to be areas of fairly great activity. However, Li also concluded that some work was proceeding in ecology, morphology, and cytology. A serious problem facing the field of botany at the time was the small number of well-trained specialists, almost all of whom had been trained in the West.

Prior to the Cultural Revolution, there were two major journals reporting on work in botany, the *Acta Botanica Sinica* and the *Acta Phytotaxonomica Sinica,* both of which have resumed publication. Plant physiology and taxonomy were the major concerns of these journals up to the Cultural Revolution. Since the resumption of publication, taxonomic studies have tended to be confined largely to the *Acta Phytotaxonomica Sinica* and have consisted of long descriptions, primarily of higher plants.

The survey of papers since the Cultural Revolution, most of which appear in the *Acta Botanica Sinica,* indicates some shift in the types of research being carried on in the field. Thus, of a total of sixty-one papers, twenty (about 31 percent) dealt with plant growth and plant

---

[3] Hui-lin Li, "Botanical Sciences," in ibid., pp. 184–87.

growth substances, while there were seven purely physiological studies, seven studies relating to plant pathology, five morphological studies, five cytological studies, four studies on plant products and drugs, and four environmental and ecological studies. There were also four taxonomic studies, one on fresh-water algae, and five studies within the area of paleobotany.

In general, it can be said that studies in botany are largely practical in orientation and tend to be directed toward support of agricultural production. This is true of most, although not all, of the physiological and cytological studies as well.

Genetics. Of the biological sciences, genetics has suffered most from political influences, having been subject to the same sort of prejudices as Soviet biology. The views of Michurin and Lysenko were prominent in China in the 1950s, although with the lessening of Soviet influence following the withdrawal of Russian scientists in the latter part of the decade, Lysenkoism gradually died out. In any event, genetics and plant breeding have been closely associated in China and genetics has been seen to be of value in its more applied and practical aspects. As a result, genetics does not appear to be at as high a level of development as it is in the West or as other biological sciences are in China.

Papers in genetics are for the most part presented in the *Acta Genetica Sinica* and the *Bulletin of Genetics (I-ch'uan-hsüeh T'ung-hsün)*. Of a total of twenty-nine papers surveyed, fifteen (about 52 percent) dealt with plant breeding. There were four papers each in areas of general genetics, cytogenetics, and medical genetics, and two papers on animal breeding.

Although there were no journals of genetics before the Cultural Revolution, genetics research was reported in *Chinese Agricultural Sciences, Science Bulletin (K'o-hsüeh T'ung-pao)*, and the *Acta Biologiae Experimentalis Sinica*. Studies at that time were concerned with plant breeding and development of new strains of plants, with some work going on in developmental and cytological genetics.

As a whole, the current studies appear to be largely concerned with the practical applications of genetics, particularly in the agricultural sciences.

Microbiology. Development within the field of microbiology has been largely concentrated in medical microbiology, particularly the study of agents involved in bacterial, viral, and parasitic diseases. In some instances, massive programs of research appear to have been launched on specific topics, such as Japanese B encephalitis and other forms of encephalitis studied extensively in the late 1950s.

Of fifty-four articles in the last two issues (February and May) of the *Acta Microbiologica Sinica* of 1966, thirty-seven (about 68 percent) were in the fields of medical microbiology and virology, ten were in immunology and serology, and two related to industrial microbiology.

Of sixty-four papers surveyed during the period since the Cultural Revolution, nineteen (about 30 percent) dealt with research in mycology, usually with reference to medically important fungi. Studies in industrial microbiology, virology, and enzymology accounted for seven papers each, while six papers were concerned with medical microbiology. There were five papers within the area of immunology and serology and three papers each on general microbiological and bacteriological topics.

Clearly, the overall trend in research in the biological sciences is toward applied biology, with emphasis on studies that are relevant to agriculture and medicine. Little work of a purely theoretical bent has been going on, and virtually none that could be considered to be at the frontiers of modern biological science. Many American and Western journals report studies much like those in their Chinese counterparts, particularly in such areas as taxonomy, general medical entomology, and general botany, but aside from such studies Chinese and Western journals share little common ground. To name a few areas in which active work is going on in the West but in which little appears to be developing in China, one might cite behavioral and physiological studies of the invertebrates, marine biology in general and phytoplankton in particular, genetics of mutation, DNA studies, molecular biology, and membrane biology.

What is of crucial importance, however, is that before the Cultural Revolution Chinese biologists were moving rapidly toward types and levels of research comparable to those in the West in a number of fields, as is shown, for example, by the paper on the application of electron microscopy to the localization of proteins on the myofibril that appeared in the *Acta Biochimica et Biophysica Sinica* in 1964 (vol. 5, no. 3). What has happened is quite simply that basic research in biology has been sacrificed to more practical concerns.

Confirmation of this view, which is based purely on the written record, comes from a number of American scientists who have traveled to China since 1971. Ethan Signer and Arthur W. Galston state that research in the biological sciences in the institutes and laboratories that they visited was largely applied and that "all biological scientists we met who were formerly doing basic research are now doing applied work and 'participating in production.'" Signer and Galston went on to say:

> Fossil and evolutionary botanists are now working on the geobotany of pollen grains, useful in petroleum prospecting; taxonomists are now concentrating on industrially useful bacterial and medically useful plant strains; bacterial geneticists formerly doing pure research are now developing new strains with better growth characteristics and high yield for industry; entomologists have switched from physiological studies to combating plant pests; and botanists who were studying basic plant physiology are now working to increase agricultural production.[4]

Another case cited by Signer and Galston was that of the insulin group at the Institute of Biochemistry in Shanghai who synthesized bovine insulin in 1965 but who are now "adapting the methodology to the industrial synthesis, for medical use, of the small peptide hormones oxytoxin and angiotensin."

In essence, then, China's scientific and political managers have effected a reorientation of priorities in the development of Chinese biological science that is more thorough-going than anything they had succeeded in doing before the Cultural Revolution. Their emphasis on applied research has resulted in a regression from the level of sophistication that existed prior to the Cultural Revolution.

Medical Research. It is in medical research that the most striking shifts in policy can be seen. Before the Cultural Revolution, in addition to the more clearly clinical journals, there were several journals reporting consistently on basic biomedical research. These were the *Acta Physiologica Sinica*, the *Acta Biologiae Experimentalis Sinica*, the *Acta Anatomica Sinica*, and the *Acta Pharmaceutica Sinica*. Work was progressing at a basic level on a wide variety of fronts, with numerous studies on experimental tumors and other forms of cancer. Following the Cultural Revolution these journals have not reappeared and with

---

[4] Ethan Signer and Arthur W. Galston, "Education and Science in China," *Science,* vol. 175 (7 January 1972), pp. 15–23. Much of what Signer and Galston report is corroborated in *China: Science Walks on Two Legs* (New York: Discus Books, 1974), pp. 109–64.

them has disappeared most mention of the sorts of basic biomedical research with which they were concerned.

It is thus clear that the charge made in the *Chinese Journal of Internal Medicine* of April 1966 (see pp. 10–11) that research on hepatitis had put too much stress on experimental research and not enough on prevention and cure was a true indication of the shift in medical research policy that was brewing at the time. A good example of this shift in priority can be seen in the handling of schistosomiasis. If one were to examine the research record on this topic, one might conclude that it was not a matter of high priority. In actuality, however, there has been a long-standing national campaign to eliminate the disease. Rather than indulging in laboratory studies that might not bear immediate fruits, the Chinese have chosen to mobilize the population to eliminate the snails that are the intermediate hosts of the causative organism. This tactic frees the research institutes to work on problems for which more immediate solutions might be found.

As a survey of the 1973 issues of the *Chinese Medical Journal* shows, most studies are of a clinical nature. Research itself is directed at a limited number of areas, including acupuncture, traditional Chinese drugs, and limb replantation. A sampling of the *Chinese Medical Journal* for 1974 suggests that this pattern is remaining relatively constant. Of the fourteen articles in the January issue, one dealt with small vessel anastamosis using dogs, a study clearly related to limb replantation, and one dealt with the efficacy and toxic effects of a new organophosphate insecticide. In the April issue, there were eighteen major papers, only two of which were not concerned with case reports or techniques. The June issue saw a somewhat higher proportion of nonclinical reports. There were papers on *Paragonimus*-induced hepatic damage involving a combination of animal experiments, autopsy, and clinical case reports, as well as a study of the effects of heating on spermatogenesis in the rabbit. There was in addition an experimental study of the peripheral afferent pathway under acupuncture anesthesia using human subjects and a study of the chemical structure of a phlorogucinol derivative isolated from the root of a Chinese herb.

Thus, the nonclinical studies have had a largely practical orientation and have very often been concerned with limb replantation problems and questions related to acupuncture physiology and traditional Chinese drugs. The practical and essentially clinical orientation of Chinese medical studies stands in stark contrast to the high proportion of basic studies reported in American journals. Such journals as *In-*

vestigative Ophthalmology, Transplantation, Pediatric Research, and *Brain Research,* to mention just a few titles, have no counterparts in China and moreover deal primarily with basic medical research. In sum, Chinese medicine is following a largely different course from that of Western medicine, a course that entirely neglects wide areas of basic research.

The Earth Sciences. Under this heading, we will consider developments in paleontology, geology, and meteorology.

Paleontology. While active publication in paleontology has resumed since the Cultural Revolution, only one of the two journals in the field, *Vertebrata Palaseatica,* has reappeared, with no evidence as yet of the *Acta Palaeontologica Sinica.* The latter, which frequently published papers originating from the Institute of Geology and Paleontology, was devoted almost exclusively to invertebrate paleontology. Thus, in terms of published papers at least, paleontology in China has become primarily vertebrate paleontology, most of the papers originating from the Institute of Vertebrate Paleontology and Paleoanthropology. None of the authors who contributed articles on invertebrate paleontology in 1966 has published since the Cultural Revolution.

Geology. In the 1950s there was a rapid expansion of geological institutes in China, the Russians were helping to train geologists, and the requirements of economic development were prompting active exploration of the nation's mineral resources. By the early 1960s efforts to gather geologic field data were increasing, but basic scientific research in geology was only beginning to be pursued.[5]

Following the Cultural Revolution, it was observed that "most provincial geological bureaus spend approximately 95 percent of their effort in searching for ores and tasks related to production and only 5 percent on research."[6] The same observer went on to say that the "principal activities of the Institute of Geology are directly in support of production," while "geological research is generally subordinate." He also indicated that since the earthquakes that occurred in 1966 at Hsingtai, south-southwest of Peking, a great deal of the work of the Institute of Geology had been devoted to "studies related to earthquake

---

[5] E. C. T. Chao, "Progress and Outlook of Geology," in *Sciences in Communist China,* p. 516.

[6] E. C. T. Chao, "Contacts with Earth Scientists in the People's Republic of China," *Science,* vol. 179 (9 March 1973), pp. 961–63.

prediction" and that 60 percent of their effort in 1972 was in that field. "Earthquake prediction is a program involving some 10,000 trained personnel (including those monitoring water levels in wells and reading earthquake instruments)."

The literature, which is presented primarily in the four journals, *Scientia Geologica Sinica, Acta Geologica Sinica, Acta Geophysica Sinica,* and *Geochimica,* and occasionally in *Science Bulletin* and *Scientia Sinica,* tends to bear out this view.

Of eighty-three studies, thirty-one (somewhat over 37 percent) can be classed within the field of seismology, while twenty-nine deal with general mineralogy, crystallography, and geochemistry. In addition, there were thirteen studies in tectonics, stratigraphy, and other structural research and ten papers dealing with historical geology, paleogeography, and similar studies. It thus appears that the major emphasis in geology at present is on earthquake research and areas that in one way or another are applicable to mineral exploration.

Further evidence of a considerable effort in geology was the All-China Symposium on Rock-Ore Analysis held at Kweiyang from 25 October to 6 November 1973. At the symposium, which was sponsored by the Chinese Academy of Sciences, the Ministry of Metallurgical Industry, and the Bureau of Geology of the State Planning Commission, 424 papers were presented on such topics as rare-earth element analysis, rock-ore analysis, electrochemical analysis, spectroscopic analysis, and atomic absorption analysis.

The first issue of *Geochimica* of 1973 contained an article entitled "The Problem of Environmental Pollution and the Mission of Earth Science Workers," which stated that the necessity for research on problems of environmental pollution requires a spirit of cooperation and an active cross-fertilization among the earth sciences, the biological sciences, and medicine. There is some evidence that this portends a more active concern with environmental research in China (see pp. 57–60).

Thus, at present, the main areas of emphasis are studies of seismicity that may lead to statistical or semiempirical approaches to earthquake prediction, studies of mineral ore deposits for the purpose of exploration for minerals, and structural studies related to tectonics. The level of work in these areas appears to be nearly the same as or possibly somewhat inferior to that in the United States and Japan. However, there seem to be few studies in certain areas related to earthquake prediction such as rock mechanics, analyses of earthquake source mechanisms, and tectonic and structural studies in relation to active fault systems. Work in these fields is at its beginning stages among Chinese earth scientists.

The research record also indicates that basic studies may be at their beginning stages in the fields of earthquake source mechanisms, tectonophysics (rock mechanics, geothermy, and so on), geomagnetism and paleomagnetism, petrology and petrochemistry (igneous, metamorphic, and sedimentary), and isotope geology (rubidium-strontium and lead-lead methods).

Among areas not being covered, or at least not being emphasized, by present research, are purely basic studies of little economic import, highly technical studies requiring specialized techniques or tools, large-scale studies requiring large numbers of highly trained scientists, large amounts of money and long periods of time, and composite or synthetic studies.[7]

Earthquake prediction in particular is an area in which mass involvement has been elicited in the form of observation of well water levels and changes in animal behavior and of instrumental observations, particularly by students in middle schools.

The relative specialization of the journals devoted to the earth sciences is a strong indication of the importance placed on geological studies. Nevertheless, even in such high-priority fields as seismology and mineralogy there is less evidence of publication than in Japan, where several journals are devoted to seismology and mineralogy. It thus appears that geology in China is at a stage in which special topics are being highlighted because of their importance for economics and public welfare.

Meteorology. In the field of meteorology there has been not so much a shift in emphasis—for the primary concern of meteorology in China has always been weather prediction—but a shift in approach. Several papers published as early as 1966 emphasized gathering information about local weather patterns from farmers in the countryside; by now Chinese meteorology relies heavily on data gathered at the local level.

Although the *Acta Meteorologica Sinica* has not been reissued following the Cultural Revolution, papers on meteorological research appear occasionally in *Scientia Sinica* and *Science Bulletin*. From 1972

---

[7] The author is indebted to Dr. Naoyuki Fujii of Tokyo University for assistance in the evaluation of the state of geology in China on the basis of the available literature.

through June 1974 eleven such papers were published, most of which were concerned with research related to weather prediction. A good percentage of the research was reported from regional weather stations, often in collaboration with the Central Weather Bureau, university departments, or other institutes.

In general, however, it appears that research has been subordinated to the immediate need for accurate prediction. There have been reports of the establishment of meteorological stations and networks for weather forecasting and observation throughout the nation. In Fukien Province, for example, it has been reported that each county has a "weather office" and that many communes have weather observation posts.[8] At the provincial level, computers may be in use in a number of areas. In Shensi Province, at least, a "China-made electronic computer" has been in service for statistical forecasting since 1973; radar instruments are being used for observations of "wind and rain" and "many county stations have applied the method of statistical forecasting in daily weather analysis and forecasting work."[9] Another approach at the local level has been that of making artificial rain and dispersing hailstorms on an "experimental basis." This was reported from Liaoning Province where more than 7,000 "hailstorm prevention points" are said to exist "throughout the province."[10]

All of this suggests that scientists and technicians trained in meteorology may have been in large part diverted from laboratory research to the practical application of their knowledge at the local level. In any event, the science of meteorology is being exploited primarily for its practical applications.

Chemistry. According to a survey of chemistry during the first decade after the revolution made by Arthur J. Yu, by 1960 chemistry in China had not reached international standards in spite of the fact that considerable work had been done in organic chemistry, which Yu considered to be the "most active field," as well as in physical chemistry, inorganic and analytic chemistry, biochemistry, and polymer chemistry. This, Yu found, was primarily because "emphasis in research has been on practical utility, and the aim of research has been to develop the chemical industry."[11] The period from 1961 to 1966 appears to have

---

[8] People's Liberation Army Fukien Front Radio, 20 February 1973.
[9] Shensi Provincial Service, 23 June 1974, Sian.
[10] Shenyang Provincial Service, 5 October 1973.
[11] Arthur J. Yu, "Chemistry," in *Sciences in Communist China*, p. 670.

been a time of considerable advance in chemistry, and in organic and biochemistry in particular, with the publication of many studies of quality comparable to that of studies appearing in Western journals, although there remained as before a heavy emphasis on applied studies. The flourishing of chemistry during the early 1960s is attested to by the existence of such journals as the *Acta Biochimica et Biophysica Sinica, Chemistry Bulletin (Hua-hsüeh T'ung-pao), Acta Chimica Sinica, Polymer Communications (Kao-fen-tzu T'ung-hsün)*, and the *Acta Pharmaceutica Sinica*, the last of which published numerous studies on amino acid synthesis. As noted previously, the paper describing the synthesis of bovine insulin was without doubt the crowning achievement of Chinese biochemists prior to the Cultural Revolution.

Since the Cultural Revolution, papers in the field of chemistry have been appearing in *Scientia Sinica, Science Bulletin,* and *Chemistry Bulletin* (this last did not begin publication until January 1974).

Of thirty-seven papers surveyed, ten (27 percent) dealt with the application of chemistry to problems of environmental pollution, perhaps a reflection of a call from the political sector for more attention to pollution on the part of scientists. There were nine articles each within the areas of industrial or applied chemistry and analytical chemistry, and eight in the field of polymer chemistry. There were an additional six articles touching on aspects of physical chemistry, two articles on the chemistry of solutions, and three articles on miscellaneous topics.

Most of the work appears to be of an applied nature, and, as suggested earlier, there seems to have been a regression from the previous advanced level of work in biochemistry in particular. While work is going on in about the same fields of chemistry as before the Cultural Revolution, there has been a decrease in the volume of published papers, which can in part be accounted for by the turn away from advanced studies in basic biochemistry. It may also be related to the trend away from basic research in medicine.

Physics. During the first decade after the Cultural Revolution work progressed in both nuclear and solid state physics. Within the realm of nuclear physics, there were studies of nuclear binding energy and spectroscopy, nuclear shell models, collective models, nuclear charge distribution, work in theoretical nuclear physics, experimental work on strange particles, studies of scattering and dispersion relations, and studies on quantum mechanics and field theory. T. Y. Wu, who sur-

48

veyed the field, came to the conclusion that, although the "volume of research is not large, most of it is connected with the latest developments in the specific fields in Western countries, and although not sensational, it is of high quality." Wu also noted that the work in the field originated from "a few small groups centered around a few (five or six) men."[12]

Beyer, who surveyed the work in solid state physics during the same period, reported that studies in that branch of physics were largely concerned with discussions of the "production of first-class materials and instruments" rather than with more advanced matters. According to Beyer, the primary area of concentration was the complex of problems associated with steel; this focus he attributed to the emphasis on heavy industry and to the "necessarily practical direction that experimental work in solid state is taking."[13] Work at that time was progressing in metals, spectroscopy, semiconductors, magnetism, acoustics and ultrasonics, electron optics, and electricity and plasticity.

The primary journal for reporting work in physics up to the Cultural Revolution was the *Acta Physica Sinica.* Since publication resumed, there have been two journals concerned with physics, the *Acta Physica Sinica,* which reappeared in 1974, and *Physics (Wu-li),* which began publication in 1972. Papers in physics also appear in *Science Bulletin.*

Of sixty-six papers published during the period surveyed, twenty-four (36 percent) were in the area of nuclear physics and thirty (close to 46 percent) were in solid state physics. There were five papers on aspects of astrophysics and cosmology and seven papers dealing with equipment and techniques and with spectrographs in particular. The primary areas of emphasis in nuclear physics appear to be neutron and neutron emission studies, scattering and shell models, strange particles, quantum theory, and field theory. In solid state physics, concentration is on microwave and laser studies, acoustics, properties of alloys and metals, spectrography, and the electron structures of chemical compounds.

Some caution must be exercised in drawing the conclusion from the published record that it tells the whole story of physics research, particularly since there are scientists engaged in research connected with the development of atomic weapons whose work obviously has not

---

[12] T. Y. Wu, "Nuclear Physics," in ibid., p. 640.
[13] Robert T. Beyer, "Solid State Physics," in ibid., pp. 649–50.

been reported in the scientific journals. Thus, we can assume that there is a considerable body of research of which we are not aware and the results of which are reported only to small groups of atomic physicists and government officials.

In this connection, it should be noted that no affiliations were listed for the authors of eleven of the papers, four of which were in the field of particle physics. A similar situation prevailed before the Cultural Revolution, when the affiliations of thirty-nine (52.7 percent) out of seventy-four authors publishing in the *Acta Physica Sinica* in 1966 were not listed or were listed merely as Chinese Academy of Sciences, suggesting that many physicists may hold "sensitive" positions.

The major centers of research in physics appear to be the Physics Institute and the Atomic Energy Institute, which accounted for twenty-nine (about 41 percent) of the papers published. The Physics Department of Peking University was relatively active, accounting for four papers.

In short, then, research in both applied and theoretical physics is proceeding rather vigorously.

Mathematics. As pointed out by Marshall H. Stone, who surveyed the field, during the first decade of the People's Republic of China mathematics was largely derivative and dependent on a relatively small number of mathematicians.[14] The best contributions were in the fields of theory of analytical functions, number theory, differential geometry, and topology. Stone also indicated a considerable emphasis on applied mathematics and ventured the prediction that within about twenty years (by 1980) China would "establish a truly independent and well-rounded mathematical activity of unimpeachable quality."[15]

Since the Cultural Revolution, papers on mathematics have been appearing primarily in two journals, the *Acta Mathematica Sinica* and *Application and Knowledge of Mathematics* (*Shu-hsüeh ti Shih-chien yü Jen-shih*), the latter devoted entirely to applied mathematics. Papers on mathematics also appear in *Scientia Sinica* and *Science Bulletin*. Of fifty-four papers published since the Cultural Revolution, twenty-one (or 39 percent) appeared in *Application and Knowledge of Mathematics*. Most of the papers in that journal were concerned with the application of mathematics to industrial problems. The topics given

---

[14] Marshall H. Stone, "Mathematics, 1949–60," in ibid., pp. 617–30.
[15] Ibid., p. 626.

primary emphasis in the *Acta Mathematica Sinica* were number theory, theory of analytic functions, differential geometry, and topology. Most of these studies were judged by one mathematician to be at a largely applied level, although one paper on probabilistic-analytical methods in denumerable Markov process was on a pure level.[16] The work presented in another paper on a "large number represented as a sum of a prime number not exceeding the product of two primes" was felt by the same mathematician to be the best solution to a well-known problem. On the other hand, Hua Lo-keng, long considered China's leading mathematician, does not seem to have been engaging in innovative mathematical studies.

It appears, then, that mathematics in China is proceeding along much the same lines as before the Culture Revolution. Recent visitors to China have been of the opinion that the emphasis has remained on applied research, although by the spring of 1973 there was an apparent shift in the direction of basic research. It is felt that the level of work in mathematics in China is below that in the United States, Europe, the Soviet Union, and Japan, but that, nevertheless, there is a potential for research at the most sophisticated level and that the Chinese are capable of making real contributions to higher mathematics if they direct their efforts in the appropriate directions. The major obstacle, in mathematics as in other disciplines, is the general orientation of the sciences toward applied work.

Astronomy. During the period from 1953 to 1960, a good number of papers of high quality were published in the field of astronomy. However, many of the papers from that period were "concerned with rather routine work such as determination of latitudes and longitudes, observations of sunspots and solar flares, photographic observations of minor planets, and improvement of orbital elements of minor planets" —the sort of studies that, "under competent supervision, could be carried out by undergraduate or graduate students or by observing assistants."[17]

By 1965 work was still proceeding along the same lines as in the period up to 1960. A notable achievement of 1965 was the discovery of the two comets Tsuchinshan 1 (1965b) and Tsuchinshan 2 (1965c) at the

---

[16] The author is indebted for the assessments of mathematics in China to Professor Kai-Lai Chung of the Department of Mathematics, Stanford University. The judgments in the remainder of the paragraph are also based on Professor Chung's appraisal.

[17] Frank Bradshaw Wood, "Astronomy," in *Sciences in Communist China*, p. 671.

Purple Mountain Observatory near Nanking. Great attention was also paid in 1965 to the observation of planets and asteroids, and three papers related to aspects of space flight were published, one on the design of the reentry orbit of a manned spaceship and one on impact and reconnaissance trajectories of a lunar vehicle. The major centers of research in astronomy over the period 1963–65 were the Purple Mountain Observatory, the various branches of the Shanghai Observatory, and Peking Observatory.

Since the resumption of publication, papers in astronomy have been appearing in the *Acta Astronomica Sinica* and occasionally in *Science Bulletin* and *Scientia Sinica*. Major areas of consideration seem to be, as they were before the Cultural Revolution, the determination of latitudes and longitudes, solar observations, orbits of comets, studies of equipment, and discussions of cosmological theory. While some papers, like one dealing with black holes, are clearly up to date, in at least one case a recently published paper was based on data collected at a much earlier time. This was an article on the variable stars in the globular cluster M79, which analyzed nine plates taken during the period 1957–58. Another paper on the spectrum of the "nitrogen flash" in the new star in Hercules apparently deals with phenomena observed in 1963.[18] This raises the question of whether research in astronomy is as active as it was before the Cultural Revolution. Publication, certainly, is still at a lower level than in the 1963–66 period. Thus, while work in astronomy has resumed, from the standpoint of volume of publication astronomy appears to be at the bottom of the list as far as priority is concerned. On the other hand, it is always possible that a good number of astronomers are contributing to the development of a Chinese space program of some kind. Here, as in physics, the published record may be deceptive.

General Summary and Evaluation

While one of the goals set for the Chinese Academy of Sciences near the beginning of the Cultural Revolution was to "catch up with and surpass world levels in scientific and research work," the overall effect of the Cultural Revolution has been to turn the better part of the effort

---

[18] The paper on black holes appeared in *Science Bulletin* (*K'o-hsüeh T'ung-pao*), vol. 19, no. 1 (1974); the other two papers were published in *Acta Astronomica Sinica*, vol. 15, no. 1 (1974).

in the sciences away from basic research to applied research.[19] Since research during the first decade after 1949 was largely applied and basic studies rose in prominence only in the years immediately preceding the Cultural Revolution, this shift suggests a reversion to an earlier pattern of scientific development. The policy that China's leaders appear to have adopted toward the sciences is a preeminently practical one: to apply the sciences to the ends of national development and to forego what for them is the luxury of solving fundamental problems on the frontiers of modern science. The biological sciences have come to function largely as a support to agriculture and to the public health sector, while the earth sciences are concerned with matters of weather prediction, mineral exploration, and earthquake prediction. The work in vertebrate paleontology is an exception, of course, one that may be permitted in the hope that prestigious discoveries will be made. Similarly, chemistry and mathematics are largely oriented toward practical ends. In nuclear physics and astronomy, on the other hand, some of the work that is going on has no immediate practical relevance beyond its prestige value.

It must also be borne in mind that there are undoubtedly areas of research related to nuclear weapons or missile development, and possibly to general space programs, about which we can learn nothing either from the literature or from visitors' reports. In any event, there are some peculiar lacunae. For instance, the published literature supplies no evidence either of the continued existence of the Institute of Metallurgy or of research in that field, yet metallurgy would certainly have considerable relevance to missile development. The Institute of Computing Technology was the source of only one paper during the period surveyed and there have been no signs of the reappearance of the *Acta Electronica Sinica* and the *Acta Automatica Sinica*. These facts taken together might suggest a considerable diversion of manpower to classified projects in the missile and space fields.

Finally, the connection between education and scientific development must not be forgotten. The Cultural Revolution was a period of great disruption in education during which there was a revolt against "elitist" standards of evaluation, with the result that when schools reopened political reliability became a more important factor in university

---

[19] The goal of catching up with and surpassing world levels was one of the ten tasks of the proletarian revolutionaries in the Chinese Academy of Sciences as outlined by Wang-Hsi-peng in his address on 30 July 1967. See pp. 14–15.

admissions than academic grades and background. Both undergraduate and graduate education suffered during the period and there can be little doubt that a serious gap remains in the supply of highly trained scientists capable of conceiving and directing research projects.

At this writing, both educational and scientific policy in China appear to be at a critical juncture. The apparent victory of the radical leftists, which has resulted in the elevation of Hua Kuo-feng to the office of premier and the removal of Teng Hsiao-p'ing with the blessing of Mao, may have signalled a renewed emphasis on political reliability as a criterion for admission to advanced education as well as an even closer integration of scientific research with the needs of agriculture and industry.

The sciences in China, then, are very likely to continue to emphasize applied over basic studies. The dislocations in education and scientific training that arose during the period of the Cultural Revolution will probably serve as a damper on development at anything comparable to the world level for several years to come, and this disadvantage will be exacerbated as the older generation of Western-trained scientists gradually passes from the scene. Furthermore, if the current politically oriented educational policies continue to be dominant—which now seems to be the most likely possibility, for the short term at least—there is the serious danger that the level and sophistication of the sciences may continue to fall.

3
Levels of Political Influence on the Sciences

In the preceding chapters, we have sought to gain an overall view of the ways in which the political sector of the society exerts control over scientific research as well as a general picture of the actual state of research in the major disciplines. It should perhaps be obvious from a comparison of both rhetoric and policy with the actual research record that the various disciplines have not been equally affected by the order to turn all scientific research toward utilitarian goals and toward national construction.

In looking at what has happened to academic disciplines in general in China since 1949, we might hypothesize a continuum of increasing political domination over intellectual endeavor running from the abstract sciences to the humanities, with the least effects being felt in those sciences that deal purely with the physical world and not with man. According to this hypothesis, as we move along the continuum from the physical toward the biological sciences, which deal with matters closer to life and livelihood, the influence of political considerations deepens. Moving further along to psychology and the social sciences, which deal with the mind of man and his relations to society, even stricter controls are applied, until with the Cultural Revolution such disciplines as anthropology, sociology, and psychology are virtually abandoned. Such a hypothetical continuum of political influence over intellectual pursuits, of course, should be applicable to the United States or the Soviet Union as well.

Apart from this general connection, however, there appear to be three levels at which the sciences in China have been subject to pressures from the political sector of the society: (1) direction of research and proportional distribution of research among fields, (2) methodology and content of research, and (3) theoretical interpretation and the history and philosophy of science.

Direction and
Distribution of Research

The direction of research, or the isolation of problems for study, has been the aspect of scientific research most directly affected by pressure from the political sector. Actual changes of direction have taken place for the most part in fields in which the proportion of basic research had been growing; these fields have reverted to predominantly utilitarian studies. Fields in which research was primarily utilitarian to begin with have been less affected. Thus, work in the biological sciences has become more closely allied than before the Cultural Revolution with problems of agriculture and medicine and less concerned with molecular biology and other studies without immediate practical application. Biochemists have turned from advanced studies on synthesis of organic compounds and from studies of cancer at the laboratory level to more mundane uses of their knowledge. Mathematicians have come to devote themselves to the solution of engineering and industrial problems.

On the other hand, there appears to have been little change in the work of meteorologists, whose main concerns have always been the practical problems of weather prediction, although their efforts have been supplemented by a mass approach to data collection. In some cases, research has been stimulated by a direct call from the leadership. For instance, in geology the considerable effort devoted to the study of earthquakes and earthquake prediction was generated by the importance attached to such work by Chairman Mao himself. Again, in medicine it was Chairman Mao's personal concern about schistosomiasis that led, not to research programs, but to mass programs aimed at exterminating the snails that are hosts to the parasite. This last instance is also a clear example of the willingness of the Chinese leadership to involve the masses in problem solving rather than to engage in long and uncertain research.

One factor that should certainly be taken into consideration is what might be called the prestige factor. This is illustrated by the work in vertebrate paleontology, which has been flourishing but which does not serve immediate utilitarian ends. The rich harvests of fossils that are yet to be discovered in China make vertebrate paleontology an area in which Chinese scientists can be expected to make valuable contributions, thus increasing China's prestige in the scientific community and providing evidence both at home and abroad that China is "catching up with and surpassing" world levels of sophistication in the sciences. Another good example is the field of particle physics, which is perhaps the most exciting and controversial area of physics at the present time. Particle physics has no immediately practical applications, but no nation aspiring to scientific greatness could afford to be without scientists working in this field. Thus it seems that scientists working in fields that carry an international prestige value and that are, as well, relatively abstruse do not suffer political pressures to alter their research programs as extreme as the pressures brought to bear on workers in other disciplines.

The distribution of research among major disciplines, at least as far as the publishing record shows, also seems to be related to the major goals of national development, with work in the biological and geological sciences overshadowing that in other fields. These two fields, of course, directly support agricultural and industrial development. Physics is next in line. Because of the gaps in our information, we do not know what the proportional balance is between these fields and the work on atomic weapons and missiles that is certainly in progress. Again, volume of publication may not be a completely reliable guide to the proportion of the national budget devoted to various disciplines, particularly since work in physics requires far more expensive equipment than that employed in the sort of biological studies that are now predominant.

The interplay between the political and the scientific media shows beyond a doubt that the locus of control over the direction of research resides in the political sector. Articles devoted to science policy in the party journal *Red Flag* are often echoed by articles as well as research reports on the relevant topics in scientific journals. An interesting example of this process concerns the question of research on environmental pollution. The December 1973 issue of *Red Flag* carried an article entitled "Protecting the Environment and Developing Production," which presented a statement of position on the topic of pollution that we must assume reflected the official line:

Protecting the environment and preventing pollution of the environment by the waste gases, waste liquids, and waste sediments given off from industrial production and actively

57

utilizing them to develop production and in the service of improving the livelihood of the people are beneficial in raising the health of the people, in promoting the development of the national economy, in consolidating the alliance between industry and agriculture, and in consolidating the dictatorship of the proletariat.

The writer then turns to the question of how to deal with the "three wastes," as the three types of waste products listed above are designated. Here he applies the principles of dialectical analysis, pointing out that the "three wastes" are no exception to the law of "dividing one into two," the technique of looking at both the positive and negative aspects of a situation, for the "three wastes" can on the one hand pollute the environment but on the other can be utilized for beneficial purposes: harmful substances can become beneficial substances. One example he cites is that of sulphur dioxide, which is given off by nonferrous metal smelting plants and which can be utilized in the production of sulphur and sulphuric acid.

More important, however, the writer goes on to present a general policy statement in which the point is made that the work of protecting and preserving the environment is the joint business of all branches of science and of all sectors of society:

> Protecting the environment is a comprehensive task that requires the involvement of industry, agriculture, and forestry and many academic specialties such as physics, chemistry, biology, medicine, meteorology, geology and hydrology. It demands of us that we link together a revolutionary spirit and a scientific attitude. We have already become clear about some of the dangers of pollution, but there may be others about which we are not clear. As old pollution problems are solved, there is the possibility that new pollution will be produced as new industrial sectors and new technological processes appear. There is no simple way to solve these problems. We must without fail give emphasis to science. We must conduct constant scientific research and conscientiously develop scientific experimental activities, through experimentation gradually coming to know and control the characteristics of and the laws governing the "three wastes" and continually raising the level of our control of the "three wastes" so as to cause environmental protection work to achieve genuine results. In the course of developing scientific experimentation, such units as scientific research facilities, the planning sectors, the health system, and the uni-

versities and colleges must work in close cooperation in assuming this mission.

Here then is a policy statement on research into the problems of environmental pollution. Because it was placed in the party journal, we can assume it to have been authoritative and to have had the sanction of the highest leaders of the government. That this expression of concern from the political sector was matched by efforts on the part of the scientific community was evident in the second issue of *Chemistry Bulletin* in 1974. In an article entitled "Environmental Research and Chemical Geography," T'an Chien-an of the Institute of Geography (CAS) summed up the relevance of the field of chemical geography in the fight against pollution in the following words:

Chemical geography is a new branch of science that was established in our nation in the latter part of the 1950s. In the course of the Great Proletarian Cultural Revolution and of the criticism of the counterrevolutionary revisionist line of Liu Shao-ch'i and Lin Piao, chemical geography, like other branches of science, has undergone a vigorous development. Workers in chemical geography, under the guidance of the revolutionary line of Chairman Mao, have taken a new step forward on the road of uniting with production practice. For several years, positive action has been exerted in inquiring into the laws of geographical distribution of some regional diseases, into the causes of chemical diseases related to "climate," and on environmental protection. Through work of this kind, chemical geography has further expanded its sphere of service to production practice and, at the same time, in serving production, has also unceasingly strengthened its own theoretical foundations and has created a new road for organic chemical geographical research. Chemical geography, in the process of serving the socialist revolution and construction, on the basis of penetrating broadly into production practice, will undergo even more rapid development and will advance even more deeply and broadly.[1]

The first issue of *Chemistry Bulletin* (January 1974) also contained a paper, originating from the Institute of Chemistry, entitled "On Environmental Protection and Chemistry." The second and third issues of that same journal carried eight other papers on environmental re-

---

[1] T'an Chien-an, "Environmental Research and Chemical Geography," *Hua-hsüeh T'ung-pao*, no. 2 (23 March 1974), pp. 10–13.

search, some on detection of such pollutants as mercury, molybdenum, and arsenic in water and some on treatment of wastes containing pollutants. It is interesting to note that even in papers dealing with highly technical discussions there is reference to the application of the principles of dialectical materialism. Thus, in a paper dealing with the recovery, utilization, and treatment of waste water containing phenol, the author in his opening remarks states that substances in the actual world follow the principle of "one dividing into two" and that the terms "waste" and "treasure" are relative and under set conditions interchangeable. For example, the author argues, phenol, if simply discharged into the environment as a waste product, is an extremely harmful substance, while, if it is recovered and properly utilized, it becomes a "treasure" of great value.[2]

In any event, there was a rapid growth in environmental research in early 1974 and there can be little doubt that this was a concrete example of the responsiveness of the scientific research community to political pressures. It should be pointed out that this is not a new phenomenon, for similar means of influence were employed by the political leaders before the Cultural Revolution. In that sense, the drastic measures taken during the Cultural Revolution to control the direction of scientific research were a departure from the customary modes of control.

Methodology and Content of Research

The intrusion of the influence of the political sector into methodology was most noticeable before the Cultural Revolution in psychological research and did not present any particular problems for the natural sciences. This certainly seems to remain true today to a large extent for such disciplines as chemistry, astronomy, and the biological sciences.

The Cultural Revolution, in advocating and implementing the policy of mass experimentation, can be said to have influenced methodology in the broad sense of the term. Once a topic, such as schistosomiasis, has been singled out for emphasis, it has been attacked in many instances by the organized efforts of large numbers of people rather

---

[2] Chang Fang-hsi, "Recovery, Utilization and Treatment of Phenol-Containing Waste Water," *Hua-hsüeh T'ung-pao,* no. 2 (23 March 1974), pp. 13–21.

than by increased laboratory research. In testing new strains of plants or new insecticides, mass approaches rather than laboratory approaches have frequently been applied. The method of intensive mass data collection, as we have noted, has also been applied in weather forecasting.

These are, however, what might be called rather gross effects on methodology. There are indications that political considerations can also have some effect on how data are interpreted. Specifically, under the influence of dialectical materialism, criticism has been directed at the methods of statistical interpretation of data characteristic of the sciences in the Western world. Signs of this trend were evident in the article dating from 1966 on hepatitis research (see p. 11) in which the author stated that researchers "should not be satisfied with a percentage of average numbers but must uphold the principle of concrete analysis of concrete problems." The same aversion to statistical approaches may have been influential among younger geologists in the field of earthquake research as well.[3]

For the most concrete examples of how political ideology can affect methodology, including attitudes toward statistical analysis, we must turn to the field of psychology. That such influences are most noticeable in psychological research further suggests the greater sensitivity of the human sciences to the political sector. The examples chosen date from the winter of 1966, when the Cultural Revolution had not yet erupted but when many of the criticisms of the sciences to be fully articulated later were first given expression in the journals.

In the first issue of the *Acta Psychologica Sinica* of 1966 (February), there were four articles illustrating the intrusion of ideology into the methodology of psychological research. These papers dealt with the class nature of man's conscious activities, the naturalistic point of view in psychology, criticism and assimilation of foreign concepts in psychology, and the revolution in psychological methodology. Three of them took the form of criticisms of the views of specific Chinese psychologists.

From our point of view, the paper on "revolution in psychological

---

[3] This is not a matter on which there is hard evidence. It was the impression of one geologist who visited China in the fall of 1974 that the voices of the older geologists, who had been overshadowed by younger scientists during the Cultural Revolution, were beginning to carry more weight (personal communication to author). If this is the case, there is a strong possibility that the younger China-trained geologists may have promoted non-statistical forms of analysis.

methodology,'' by one Li Cheng, is the most revealing.[4] It is a criticism of the views of psychologist Ch'en Yuan-hui, whose major error is seen to have been to advocate the use of the experimental method and the application of mathematics in psychological research: "Method in psychology should be primarily the experimental method,'' Ch'en says. "In addition to the experimental method, mathematical method should be an important aspect of it." Li further quotes Ch'en as saying that the "use of mathematical method in psychological research should be one of the directions in psychological research'' and that the "use of formulas to express the laws of psychological activity'' should become a "direction of the efforts of psychologists.''

While such a view might put Ch'en in the mainstream of American experimental psychology, Li Cheng disapproves of it strongly. For one thing, it borrows heavily on the methodology of Western psychology. This is seen as being bad in two ways. First, Li feels that it is important for Chinese psychologists to work out their own indigenous methodology. His main objection, however, is that the methodology of Western psychology has a bourgeois class origin. As he says, "The experimental method and the mathematical method about which Ch'en Yuan-hui is talking are drawn from the 'treasury' of bourgeois class psychology.'' Li goes on to discuss why this is bad.

> We know that psychology is the study of human psychological phenomena and that the experimental method used by bourgeois psychologists cannot, fundamentally, be dissociated from the bourgeois psychologist's interpretation of the essential nature of man. The interpretation of the essential nature of man held by bourgeois psychologists is the viewpoint of "humanism" and "naturalism." This view leaves out man's social and class relationships, considering man to belong to a biological and purely natural category.

According to Li, psychology cannot be understood apart from considerations of the "social character" and "historical development of man"; Ch'en's approach fails to grasp the dependence of human phenomena on production and class struggle. Thus, "the experimental method and mathematical method of bourgeois psychology serve their viewpoint; that is, they are in the service of studying the psychology of 'natural man.' World view and methodology are consistent, and view-

---

[4] Li Cheng, "Revolution in Psychological Methodology—A Discussion with Comrade Ch'en Yuan-hui," *Acta Psychologica Sinica*, no. 1 (1966).

point, standpoint, and methodology are also unified. This is the characteristic of the experimental method, the mathematical method, and other methods of bourgeois psychology."

Li denounces Ch'en's negative attitude toward the use of class analysis in psychological research: "Class analysis," he quotes Ch'en, "is only applicable to the study of society and is a method for doing research only on social problems but cannot be used to do research on human psychological phenomena and therefore cannot be a method of psychology." Li's reply is that class analysis must be applied to problems arising from situations in which class relations and class struggle are present. "And what, after all, is the human mind? Is not the human mind the reflection of objective reality in the human brain? And are not, in a class society, class relationships and class struggle present in the objective reality reflected in the human mind and consciousness? And should we not apply the method of class analysis to the study of the origin of these problems in the human mind and consciousness?"

While we cannot be certain that the debate was not staged to stress the class and antimathematical approach to psychological research, we can be sure that it was meant to impress upon research workers in the field that there was a preferred methodology.

We have a number of examples from the period prior to the Cultural Revolution of how psychologists applied some of the approved principles to their research. Some of the most striking examples are drawn from the politically sensitive field of research on "moral education." In a paper entitled "The Principle of Class Analysis Must Be Applied to Research on the Psychology of Moral Education," the author stresses the point that the basic task in research on moral education is that of "setting the younger generation of our nation on the correct political course, accelerating their revolutionization on the basis of the five conditions of a proletarian revolutionary successor set out by Chairman Mao."[5] He concludes that since morality has a class character, psychological research on moral education must take class and class struggle into consideration:

> In a class society, morality has a class character, and the various psychological processes of adolescents and children are stamped with a class brand. Consequently, the viewpoint

---

[5] Ssu-ma Feng, "The Principle of Class Analysis Must Be Applied to Research on the Psychology of Moral Education," ibid., no. 2 (1965), pp. 114–20.

of class struggle and the methods of class analysis must be used in research on the problem of formation of moral qualities. Similarly, the standpoint of class struggle and the methods of class analysis should also be used in research on the problem of the capacity of adolescents and children for moral judgment.[6]

When we look at the reported research on moral education, we find that such considerations as these are basic. Moral behavior is evaluated in a highly political light. In a paper entitled "The Effect of Model Contrast on Self-Evaluation in School Pupils," for example, the class origins of the pupils involved in the study are noted: fifty-five of them were children of poor or lower-middle peasants, twenty the children of ordinary workers, and five the children of exploitative families. The pupils were instructed in the model behavior of the soldier Lei Feng, on the basis of which they engaged in self-criticism attempting to identify their own good and bad points. Analyzing the results of this study, the author proposes nine items that might serve as standards of judging moral virtues in children: study and use of the writings of Chairman Mao; a proletarian class viewpoint and attitude; a spirit of service to the people and a Communist style of unselfish devotion to the benefit of others and to helping others as a pleasure; a labor viewpoint and attitude; a mass viewpoint; a spirit of solidarity with comrades; a humble acceptance of mass opinion in a spirit of self-criticism; a dialectical materialist viewpoint; and a spirit of hardship, simplicity, diligence, and frugality.[7] This paper is but one of a series of studies in which both the topic and the outcome of the research were undoubtedly affected by value preferences originating in the political sector.

Aside from psychology, most fields did not suffer from this sort of political intrusion into their methodology to any great extent in the years immediately preceding the Cultural Revolution. One exception was meteorology in early 1966. In the March 1966 issue of the *Acta Meteorologica Sinica* (vol. 36, no. 1), for instance, there were a number of papers describing how professional meteorologists had adopted a new approach to local weather prediction. One of these papers, "Utilizing the Experiences of the Masses in Preparing Meteorological Weather Station Forecasts," written by members of a meteorological station in

---

[6] Ibid., p. 114.
[7] Nieh Shih-mao, "The Effect of Model Contrast on Self-Evaluation in School Pupils," ibid., no. 2 (1966), pp. 146–53.

Liaoning Province, described how the meteorologists sought out and checked the validity of popular local sayings about and ways of predicting weather.

What should be noted since the Cultural Revolution is a growing tendency for scientific writers to purport to apply the method of dialectical materialism to the solution of scientific problems. Their papers go a step beyond the passing invocation of such principles as "one dividing into two" and call for the use of the dialectic viewpoint in considering concrete problems.

A good example of this sort of paper is one entitled "Analysis of Some Problems of Electrolysis and Electroplating in the Light of Dialectics," which appeared in *Chemistry Bulletin* in early 1975.[8] The paper, by two individuals who were identified as "worker-peasant-soldier" students of the Hua Chung Engineering College, dealt with what the authors had learned from applying dialectics to an analysis of the "contradictions" in the processes of electrolysis and electroplating. While much of the paper falls within the realm of theoretical interpretation, which we will consider in a moment, the authors do have something to say about how dialectics can be applied as a method in observation. Remarking that in "electrochemical experiments, we can clearly see that the various phenomena of electrolysis and electroplating" all obey certain "basic laws" of their own, that is to say, the "law of the unity of opposites," they go on to say:

> If we observe them from a static and one-sided viewpoint, then we will see them as being eternally independent of each other and eternally invariable. When we use dialectical materialism to observe events, we find that each event has its own internal relationships, which include its own opposite and which form a unity of opposites. This is the essential relationship of matter and events. Each event also has its external relationships which lead to complex relationships with surrounding matter and events. Therefore, matter and events are constantly developing in a process going from quantitative to qualitative change, a process in which one thing is transformed into another. The basic cause of this process of quantitative to qualitative change and of the transformation of one thing into another does not lie in the external aspects of a thing, but in the internal aspects of a thing, in the internally contradictory nature of a thing.

---

[8] Chen Chuan-de and Meng Kang, "Analysis of Some Problems of Electrolysis and Electroplating in the Light of Dialectics," *Hua-hsüeh T'ung-pao*, no. 1 (1975), pp. 13–14.

The authors conclude that it is only necessary to apply the principle of the unity of opposites in experiments on electrolysis and electroplating, observing and analyzing them from a standpoint of one dividing into two, for it to be possible to come to scientific conclusions in harmony with this law. A number of examples of the application of this method to various problems are presented. One of these is how the behavior of two types of conductors differed in response to increases in temperature (an identical external cause) because of differences in internal structure (differing internal causes).

There is, of course, the possibility that papers of this sort are essentially showpieces written at the request of journal editors or of members of the revolutionary committees in the colleges and institute laboratories. In any event, they often represent a considerable cost in what must be presumed to be valuable space in the journals, and for that reason we are led to assume that they are intended to be taken very seriously by the members of the scientific community.

Since the above paper attempted to link methodology and theory, it serves as a good introduction to our next consideration, the effects of political factors on theoretical interpretation in the sciences.

Theoretical Interpretation:
History and Philosophy
of Science

The theoretical reinterpretation of scientific principles, hinted at in the paper on electrolysis quoted above, is perhaps the most interesting phenomenon to appear in the sciences in China. While this tendency has always existed, it has become far more extreme since the Cultural Revolution than it was before 1966, with discussions of scientific topics in the light of dialectical materialism appearing even in journals of chemistry and physics.

Some of the papers are simply expositions of dialectical interpretation, but others set forth propositions that are essentially repudiations of the philosophical foundations of Western science. Such a paper is "The Violent Struggle between Materialism and Idealism that Has Existed throughout the Development of Chemistry," which appeared in the March 1974 issue of *Chemistry Bulletin*. Written by members of the *Dialectics of Nature* Study Group of the Chemistry Research Group of the Central China College of Engineering, it is a report of the understandings gained from studying Engel's *Dialectics of Nature* and

66

traces the history of chemical theory from the time of the atomic theory of Democritus to modern times in terms of the struggle between materialist and idealist interpretations of chemistry. In the course of a discussion of the "struggle between materialism and idealism in the theory of molecular structure," the authors turn to the point that the Kekulé structural formulas do not, under many conditions, accurately reflect molecular structure and that they do not furnish a satisfactory explanation, for example, of all of the properties of benzene. The discussion proceeds as follows:

Beginning in the 1930s, in the twentieth century, such Americans as Pauling and Wheland proposed the "theory of resonance" as a solution to this problem. The viewpoint of the natural sciences on the "theory of resonance" is a problem requiring further investigation and is one about which there are disputes among various schools. However, there are definite tendencies to idealism and agnosticism in the epistemology of the theory of molecular structure of such persons as Pauling and Wheland. For example, Pauling, in his book, *The Nature of the Chemical Bond,* has written, "The convenience and value of the concept of resonance in studying chemical problems is exceedingly great so that the defect of its existing arbitrary element is of no matter." Wheland went on further to say that "The concept of resonance, as compared to other physical theories, is an even more profoundly artificial concept. It does not by any means reflect any internal properties of the molecule itself but is merely a mathematical approach created by physicists and chemists for their own convenience." Taking the standpoint of materialism, we must ask: Is or is not a correct theory and concept of molecular structure the reflection of an objectively existing molecular structure? If we hold that it is, then there can be no "arbitrary element" or "artificial concept." If we hold that it is not, if we hold that it is merely a "working hypothesis" established for "convenience," then this is anarchy, a viewpoint corresponding to the idealist and agnostic views on molecular structure of such persons as Dumas and Euler. This kind of idealist philosophical viewpoint can only lead one to exaggerate the relativity of the structural formula and to deny the objective reality of the object that it reflects, leading one to go around in circles of pure mathematics and to neglect to carry out research on the actual structure of a substance. The entire history of the development of the theory of molecular structure bears out that idealism and agnosticism are capable only of leading us down the wrong road and that dialectical materialism is the only correct view and theory of knowledge leading to progressive development.[9]

One of the major points made by the authors is that idealistic theories such as "vitalism" disrupt the progress of science. Once the accomplishment of the synthesis of organic chemicals had destroyed the idealistic theory of vitalism, they claim, chemistry moved forward with a "flying leap." It is clear why, viewing the history of chemistry as "the history of the struggle between materialism and idealism and the history of the struggle between materialism and metaphysics," they should take such a severe view of Pauling's and Wheland's statements on the artificial character of the "working hypothesis" of resonance. They are saying, in short, that they will not be satisfied with anything less than a final and complete concrete explanation of the nature of matter and processes in the physical world and that "working hypotheses" stand in the way of achieving this goal.

This view implies an acceptance of the concrete reality of chemical and physical concepts. As the authors comment, the atomic theory developed by Dalton "laid the materialistic theoretical foundations of chemistry." This attitude is even more clearly expressed in their comment on a statement attributed to Dumas in 1840 that he would like to throw the term "atom" out because he was convinced that it was outside of human experience. The Chinese writers comment, "Insomuch as he denied the objective existence of the object itself of chemical research, this naturally blocked the way to the forward development of chemistry." This statement reflects a more "naive" and materialistic approach to the sciences on the theoretical and philosophical levels than is common in the West.

A similar approach in genetics is to be found in a paper entitled "Chairman Mao's 'On Contradiction' and Genetic Studies" which appeared in the first issue of the *Acta Genetica Sinica*. Written by Fang Tsung-hsi of the department of biology of the Shantung College of Oceanography, the paper deals with a number of genetic problems from the standpoint of Mao's views as expressed in his famous "On Contradiction," particularly Mao's view that "in studying a problem we must shun objectivity, one-sidedness and superficiality." Mao's views and his own interpretation of genetic theory lead Professor Fang to deny

---

[9] *Dialectics of Nature* Study Group, Chemistry Research Group, Central China College of Engineering, "The Violent Struggle between Materialism and Idealism that Has Existed throughout the Development of Chemistry," ibid., no. 3 (May 1974), pp. 15–16.

the concept of the gene as a metaphysical entity and to present evidence supporting its actual existence.[10]

In his introductory paragraph, Professor Fang discusses the problem of the penetration of the capitalist world view into the science of genetics:

> In recent years, genetics, which is a branch of the natural sciences, has developed very rapidly and many accomplishments have been made in it. At the same time, it is still infused with many idealist and metaphysical concepts. Examples of this are the views that single genes produce single characteristics, that the gene is not divisible, and that the process of mutation cannot be controlled. This is understandable since modern genetics developed for the most part in capitalist nations and it is only to be expected that the capitalist world view would exert various influences on it. This is because, "In a class society, each individual lives in a definite class position and there is not one of his ideas that is not stamped with a class brand." ("On Practice" [by Mao Tse-tung]). Consequently, in dealing with genetics, we must, just as in dealing with other sciences that have been developed in capitalist societies, adopt the dialectic viewpoint of "dividing one into two" and make concrete analyses of concrete problems.

With this introduction, Professor Fang turns to specific questions within the field of genetics. Of no little interest is his application of the thought of Mao to problems of heredity and of functions within the cell. As Chairman Mao "teaches," Fang says, from the standpoint of materialist dialectics, "external causes are the conditions of change and internal causes are the basis of change, while external causes become operative through internal causes." On this basis, Fang believes that environment and heredity must be regarded as different things and that phenotype should be clearly distinguished from genotype. While he concludes that acquired characteristics cannot be inherited, he does point out that there is a genetic basis for developing acquired characteristics.

In dealing with the relationship between the nucleus and the cytoplasm, he refers to Mao's statement that "of two contradictory aspects, one must be principal and the other secondary. The principal

---

[10] Fang Tsung-hsi, "Chairman Mao's 'On Contradiction' and Genetic Studies," *Acta Genetica Sinica,* vol. 1, no. 1 (June 1974), pp. 7–15.

aspect is the one playing the leading role in the contradiction." Thus Professor Fang believes that the nucleus, which contains the chief genetic materials, must be considered the principal aspect, playing the leading role in the cell. But he also points out that, in the view of materialist dialectics, the principal and nonprincipal aspects can be transformed into each other. This is what he believes to be true of the relation between the nucleus and the cytoplasm.

One could cite from the recent scientific literature a good number of other examples of the interpretation of biological, chemical, and physical phenomena on the basis of the writings of Mao and the concepts of dialectical materialism. The March 1974 issue of the *Acta Physica Sinica* ran an article entitled "The Universe Is the Unity of Infinitude and Finiteness." Framed with quotations from Engels and Lenin, the author's thesis is that infinitude and finiteness form a unity of opposites and that the views on the infinitude and finiteness of the universe formulated throughout history, from Newton's classical model of the universe to modern cosmology, cannot lead to a correct knowledge of the dialectics of infinitude and finiteness, but instead degenerate into metaphysics and idealism.

In an editorial note preceding the article, the editors of the journal issue a call for more articles of this sort.

> It is hoped that the broad groups of physics workers are able, with self-awareness, to utilize dialectical materialism to guide their own scientific research work, and, in summing up their actual research work, to endeavor to study, use and promulgate the materialist dialectical method and to criticize idealism and metaphysics. . . . We hope that in the future we will be able to read many more good articles applying Marxism, Leninism, and the thought of Mao Tse-tung to concrete analysis of concrete contradictions in the realm of research on physics.

In 1975, at least, there was little response to this call, with only one paper of note, entitled "Heat Is a Form of Motion of Matter," dealing with the "dialectics of nature."[11] Other articles of a political nature, however, appeared in the *Acta Physica Sinica*.

As a rule, ideologically oriented theoretical or research papers have accounted for a relatively small proportion of the articles published in the major scientific journals, although as many as three or four

---

[11] *Acta Physica Sinica*, vol. 24, no. 5 (1975), pp. 237–43.

have been known to appear in the same issue. Two examples of such ideologically oriented papers from 1975 are "Applying Materialist Dialectics to Win Steady Good Harvests with Three Crops a Year"[12] and "Some Understandings from Studying the *Dialectics of Nature*—On the Origin of Reptiles."[13] Some scientific journals also publish papers on the history of science and very often on the history of the sciences in China.

Articles on the history of science appear most commonly, however, in the party journal, *Red Flag*. There were two good examples of such articles in 1973. One of them, "Viewing the Struggle between Materialism and Idealism from the Theory of Evolution," as the title suggests, outlines the historical development of the theory of evolution as a struggle between materialism and idealism and between dialectics and metaphysics.[14] The other article, "The Development of Man's Knowledge of the Universe," takes the same position.[15] A similar article, "How Did the Theory of Calculus Come into Being?" appeared in the January 1973 issue of *Red Flag*. The author traces the history of calculus from the latter half of the seventeenth century, stressing that if the concepts, judgments, and inferences that are the matter of calculus are alienated from human practice and the data obtained from the objective world, they are without foundation. The writer criticizes the "number of mathematicians and idealist philosophers" who have made a "one-sided exaggeration" of the function of abstract thinking and logical inference in mathematics:

> They denied that the objects of mathematical research are quantitative relations and space configurations. They regarded mathematics as "purely a system of deduction" and claimed that the object of mathematic research was pure "formalization of symbols." The logicism and formalism which appeared in the early 20th century represented idealist trends of this type. . . . They provided mathematics with idealist explanations and cloaked it with apriorism, trying to lead mathematics astray onto the evil road of becoming divorced from practice and of giving up imagination and intuition. This tendency was extremely detrimental to the development of mathematics.[16]

[12] *Acta Botanica Sinica,* vol. 17, no. 3 (1975), pp. 180–87.
[13] *Vertebrata Palaseatica,* vol. 13, no. 4 (1975), pp. 199–201.
[14] *Hung Ch'i,* no. 12 (1973).
[15] Ibid., no. 7 (1973).
[16] Shu Li, "How Did the Theory of Calculus Come into Being?" ibid., no. 1 (1973).

This is a fairly representative illustration of the kind of argument that is put forward about the history of the sciences. For our purposes here, it offers a sidelight on the concern of the political sector with all aspects of the sciences.

The intriguing question that arises at this point is what all this talk about applying dialectical materialism to the sciences really means. It is, in part, a manifestation of the drive toward unification of thought under a single ideology that has been an important aspect of Chinese culture for centuries. It is also a manifestation of the policy of keeping the sciences under the domination of the political sector of the society. Papers dealing with the application of dialectical materialism to scientific research do not constitute a significant proportion of the published literature, most reports dealing with practical matters. Nevertheless, the dialectical approach may be meaningful in that it could stand in the way of serious Chinese contributions to theoretical studies at the international level and in that it may represent a sincere attempt to work out a distinctive, Chinese way of dealing with basic scientific questions. Whether or not this is the case the future will decide.

4
Implications for
Scientific Cooperation and Exchange

With the "reopening" of China following President Nixon's visit and the Shanghai Communiqué of 1972, there has been a continuous stream of American visitors, many of them scientists, to the People's Republic of China. A number of scientific delegations from China have also visited the United States. The question that arises now is to what extent the high hopes for scientific and scholarly exchange raised by these developments will be fulfilled.

There is no simple or straightforward answer. Many factors affect the possibilities for scientific cooperation and exchange between the United States and China, most of which are beyond the power of the United States to influence. These factors can be classed in two broad groups, those that primarily involve political questions entirely extraneous to the sciences and those that involve the sciences either directly or indirectly. They can be summarized as follows:

(1) Political factors extraneous to the sciences
   (a) Internal political factors
   (b) International political factors
(2) Factors pertaining to the sciences
   (a) Nature and extent of past and present scientific and technical agreements and exchanges
   (b) Extent and level of intrusion of political factors into scientific work
   (c) Level of Chinese scientific work as measured by international standards
   (d) Development needs requiring application of scientific research as perceived by the Chinese and the extent to which these needs make outside assistance necessary

The nature and extent of past and present scientific and technical agreements and exchanges is, of course, a result of these factors and therefore may have some predictive value as well as giving us some indication of what the actual interplay among these factors amounts to. Let us take a look, then, at the record of China's participation in international scientific ventures and agreements.

Since the late 1950s, China has signed agreements on scientific and technical cooperation with the Soviet Union and the East European countries within the Communist sphere. As a rule, these agreements have been made between the respective academies of science of China and of the nation concerned; typical of them was the agreement between the Academy of Sciences of the People's Republic of Romania and the Chinese Academy of Sciences, signed in Peking on 6 July 1963. This agreement provided for exchange of scientific workers for the purpose of engaging in official-academic trips, studies, and "exchange of experiences," that is, exchange of information based on experiences in given matters. It stipulated provisions for invitations to scientific workers to take part in conferences in both China and Romania and stated that each side would furnish the other with information obtained at international conferences, a procedure enabling the Chinese to obtain information about the content of conferences in which they could not participate directly for international political reasons. The academies also agreed to exchange, as far as possible, publications, information, data, photographs, and microfilms necessary for scientific work, the exchange of publications to be negotiated directly by their libraries.

Under the agreement, the two academies were to send representatives by turns to Peking and Bucharest at two-year intervals or to communicate by other means for the purpose of signing two-year plans and of reviewing the state of execution of the plan currently in effect. These plans were to be approved by the Standing Committee of the Chinese Academy of Sciences and by the Presidium of the Academy of Sciences of the People's Republic of Romania. The agreement between the academies was to become effective after approval by these two bodies. The term of the agreement was six years, to be automatically extended for another six years if no written notification to the contrary was issued by either side within six months of the date of expiration.[1]

---

[1] For the complete text of the agreement see *Chung-hua Jen-min Kung-ho-kuo T'iao-yüeh-chi,* vol. 12 (Peking: Shih-chieh Chih-shih Ch'u-pan-she, 1964), pp. 217–20.

The other most common type of agreement has been in the field of public health and medicine. For example, agreements were signed between the Ministry of Public Health of the People's Republic of China and the comparable organs of the People's Republic of Poland, the People's Republic of Czechoslovakia, and the Democratic Republic of Germany in 1957. Most of these were to be effective for five years with provisions for renewal.

The agreement between the Chinese Ministry of Public Health and the Ministry of Public Health of the People's Republic of Poland was typical of these agreements. Its second clause dealt with methods for promoting exchange of experiences between public health organizations and in various aspects of medical science and contained the following items: (1) cooperation in medical science, (2) exchange of important medical literature, books, and photographs, (3) exchange of experiences in disease prevention, particularly the prevention of infectious diseases, (4) exchange of experiences on methods of treatment and manufacture of drugs, (5) exchange of medical statistics, (6) exchange of biological cultures and vaccines, and (7) exchange of public health plans and major guidelines for public health organizations of concern to the other side and of data on planned finances.

The third clause dealt with the establishment of cooperative ventures in the training of public health workers and contained the following two provisions: (1) mutual dispatch of physicians, scientific workers, and other public health personnel, and (2) exchange of outlines of teaching plans for advanced and intermediate medical colleges and schools. The agreement also allowed for mutual treatment of medical patients in the respective countries.[2]

More recently the Chinese have signed a considerable number of agreements on scientific cooperation and exchange (see Table 6). To the best of our knowledge, these agreements have not been dead letters. In the case of Romania, for instance, there have been active cultural exchanges. Chinese students in the biological and geological sciences have gone to Romania for periods of study of up to six years. The fact that students of geology have been selected for study in Romania is of particular significance in the light of Romania's rich mineral deposits and technological advances in the field of mineral exploitation.

Two additional points concerning the exchanges between China

---

[2] Ibid., vol. 6 (Peking: Fa-lü Ch'u-pan-she, 1958), pp. 229–30.

Table 6

MAJOR SCIENTIFIC AND TECHNICAL AGREEMENTS, 1973-74

Year	Agreement	Countries
With Communist bloc countries:		
1973	Protocols on scientific and technical cooperation	Czechoslovakia, Romania, Bulgaria, Democratic People's Republic of Korea, Democratic Republic of Vietnam
1973	Agreements on health cooperation	Democratic Republic of Vietnam, Romania
1974	Protocols and agreements on scientific and technical cooperation	Democratic Republic of Vietnam, Bulgaria, Czechoslovakia, Hungary, Yugoslavia, Democratic People's Republic of Korea
With non-Communist countries:		
1973	Protocols on sending Chinese medical teams	Mali, Tunisia
1974	Cooperation in medicine and health	Argentina, Sudan
1974	Agricultural cooperation	Upper Volta
1974	Agreement on permanent scientific exchange between the Chinese Academy of Sciences and the Max Planck Society	Federal Republic of Germany
1974	Preliminary agreement on a Japan-China oceanographic institute	Japan

Note: Agreements relating to the Chinese archaeological exhibition are not included.

Source: Foreign Broadcast Information Service (FBIS).

and Romania are of note. First, no senior scientists have been included in the Chinese delegation to Romania and second, very few Romanian scientists have gone to China and those few scholars who have gone have been engaged in cultural studies. The reason for this is presumably that Romanian scientists have not felt that the level of China's scientific and technological development was sufficiently high to make research trips to China particularly worthwhile.[3]

Thus, in general, China's agreements with Communist bloc countries have fallen into the two general categories of protocols on scientific and technical cooperation (many of which have been running for from thirteen to fifteen years) and agreements on cooperation in medicine and health. All of those signed in the late 1950s and early 1960s follow essentially the patterns illustrated by the agreement between China and Romania and that between China and Poland cited above.

Most of China's agreements with non-Communist nations, on the other hand, have been protocols on sending Chinese medical teams abroad and have been executed with African countries. The two major exceptions are China's agreements with the Federal Republic of Germany and with Japan. The former is an agreement between the Chinese Academy of Sciences and the Max Planck Society and provides for exchange visits by eight to ten scientists from each of the two institutes during the first year or two.[4] In addition, two to four younger Chinese scientists were to go to the Federal Republic of Germany for one to two years, German scientists were to be invited to lectures and seminars in China, and the Chinese Academy of Sciences was invited to send a delegation to Germany in October 1974. Another group, from the Scientific and Technical Association, was to go to Germany in May 1974 under the leadership of Chou Pei-yuan, head of the Scientific and Technical Association, who had worked on armaments research in the United States during the Second World War. (Subsequently, in 1975, Chou led a delegation to the United States.)

The purpose of the agreement with Japan was the establishment of a Japan-China oceanographic institute. The agreement, worked out between a Japanese mission made up of oceanographers, fishery representatives, and members of ocean development enterprises and their Chinese counterparts, was said to have been prompted by a desire on

---

[3] The information on Chinese-Romanian exchanges is based on a personal communication.
[4] NCNA, Peking, 26 April 1974; and DPA, Hamburg (Federal Republic of Germany), 26 April 1974.

the part of the Chinese to promote the exchange of scientific and technical information with Japan in the fields of fisheries and ocean development.[5]

It may be significant that these agreements relate to fields in which the Chinese stand to benefit from advanced technology. It is also of great interest that the agreement with the Max Planck Society is the only known agreement to date with a Western country calling for the prolonged absence of Chinese scientists from their country and that the scientists the Chinese plan to send to Germany on a long-term basis are "younger scientists," that is, persons who have grown up under the new regime and who can be expected to have internalized its values more thoroughly than older people, thus making them better risks for residence abroad. It will be worth noting whether or not this becomes a standard pattern under future exchange agreements permitting Chinese scientists to work abroad.

Of greatest interest from the standpoint of American scientists are the two cooperative ventures between individual American and Chinese scientists. The first of these took place in the fall of 1972 when Professor Man-chiang Niu of Temple University spent four months at the Institute of Zoology in Peking working with Dr. Tung-ti Chou, professor of biology at the Chinese Academy of Sciences. It was reported that together the two scientists had "verified for the first time through animal experiments that messenger ribonucleic acid (mRNA) isolated from cytoplasm (the protoplasm of a cell, exclusive of the nucleus) plays a significant role in cell differentiation, development, and hereditary characteristics."[6] The results of their work were reported in *Scientia Sinica*.[7]

The second cooperative venture took place in the winter of 1973 and involved Yeh Tu-cheng of the Institute of Atmospheric Physics of the Chinese Academy of Sciences and Professor Chang Cheih-ch'ien of the Catholic University of America. Professor Chang worked with Yeh at the Institute of Atmospheric Physics for a short period. The result of their cooperative effort was a paper entitled "A Preliminary Experimental Simulation of the Heating Effect of the Tibetan Plateau on the General Circulation over Eastern Asia in Summer," which appeared in *Scientia Sinica* a few months later.[8] Professor Chang subse-

[5] Kyodo, 5 December 1974, Tokyo.
[6] *China Exchange Newsletter*, vol. 16, no. 3 (Winter 1973-74), p. 4.
[7] *Scientia Sinica*, vol. 16, no. 3 (1973).
[8] Ibid., vol. 17, no. 3 (1974).

quently undertook another visit to China in the spring and the summer of 1975.

In both cases, we note, it was the American scientist who visited China and not the Chinese who came to the United States. Furthermore, the American scientists involved were both of Chinese origin, with the result that language problems were minimized. Again, it will be of interest to see whether or not these ventures set a pattern for any further joint projects that may develop. At this juncture, however, it is not clear whether there will be any further joint ventures of this kind between Chinese and American scientists, although the return of Professor Chang Chieh-ch'ien to China would seem to be propitious.

One further instance of a joint venture, this time involving a government agency rather than individual scientists, was the vist to China in the fall of 1974 by scientists of the U. S. Geological Survey, who worked with their Chinese counterparts in the field of seismology.

Joint ventures have been few, but communications have been maintained between Chinese and American scientists, certainly at the institutional level and perhaps on a personal level; no systematic information is available on this point. It goes without saying, of course, that communication between Chinese-speaking Americans and their Chinese counterparts is simpler than that between English-speaking Americans and Chinese and may be more common. In any event, communications from individuals or groups in China very often have to be made by way of the People's Republic of China Liaison Office in Washington rather than by direct contact with the American scholars concerned.

Perhaps one of the best keys for assessing Chinese interests in the area of international scientific cooperation is the composition of the groups that have traveled abroad in the period after 1972. These foreign ventures are significant both because they give us good indications of Chinese priorities and because they have furnished Chinese scientists with opportunities for personal contact with their Western counterparts. For the sake of convenience, we shall concentrate on the movements of Chinese scientists in 1973 and 1974 (see Table 7).

A considerable number of groups of Chinese scientific personnel went abroad in 1973 and 1974. These groups can be divided into three general categories: (1) medical teams working in foreign countries, (2) medical personnel and scientists making "friendly visits" abroad, and (3) medical personnel and scientists attending conferences abroad.

Table 7
CHINESE MEDICAL AND SCIENTIFIC VISITS ABROAD, 1973–74

1973

MEDICAL DELEGATIONS

Delegations to Kuwait, England, Yugoslavia, Japan, Korea, and Burma
A delegation to Mexico, Chile, and Peru
A delegation to Finland, Sweden, and Austria
A delegation to Switzerland, Thailand, and the Philippines

SCIENTIFIC DELEGATIONS

Scientific and technical delegation to Japan
Civil engineering delegation to Japan
Biologists' delegation to Japan
Zoology study group to North Korea
Seismology study group to Sweden
High energy physicists to the United States
Hydraulic engineering study group to the United States
Insect hormone group to the United States

MEDICAL CONFERENCES

Meeting of Japanese Society of Acupuncture and Oriental Medical Society in Japan
Thirty-Fifth Meeting of the Japan Clinical Surgery Society in Japan
Workshop on hepatitis B antigen in Japan
Annual scientific conference of the West African Medical Research Council in Kenya
Annual meeting of the Ethiopian Medical Association in Ethiopia
Medical advisory panels, Organization for African Unity, Ethiopia
Fourth International Seminar on Cardiac Pacemaking at The Hague
Twenty-Sixth Session of the World Health Assembly in Switzerland
Second International Symposium on Early Cancer Detection and Prevention in Italy
International Symposium on Differentiation and Function of Lymphoid Cells in Romania
Twenty-Fifth Session of the International Conference on Surgery in Spain

SCIENTIFIC DELEGATIONS

Eighth International Conference on Plant Growth Substances in Japan
Fourth International Aeronautics and Astronautics Exhibition in Japan
International Conference on Population Planning for National Welfare and Development in Pakistan
Twenty-Ninth Annual Meeting of the Ceylon Association for the Advancement of Science in Sri Lanka

Thirty-First Annual Meeting of the Plastic Engineering Society in Canada

Continental Meeting on Science and Man in Mexico

Celebrations of the 100th Anniversary of the Founding of the Prussian Geological Survey Institute in the Federal Republic of Germany

Eleventh Session of the International Conference on Large Dams in Spain

Sixth Session of the Commission for Instruments and Methods of Observation of the World Meteorological Organization in Finland

Technical Conference on the Observation and Instruments of Atmospheric Pollution (WMO-WHO) in Finland

Celebrations of the Centenary of the International Meteorological Organization/World Meteorological Organization in Austria

Twenty-Fifth Session of the World Meteorological Organization Executive Committee in Switzerland

1974

MEDICAL DELEGATIONS

Specialists in limb replantation to Canada and the United States

Delegations to Romania, Syria, Lebanon, Iraq, and Canada

SCIENTIFIC DELEGATIONS

Scientific group to West Germany, Switzerland, and France

Engineering workers delegation to England

Chemical industry delegation to Federal Republic of Germany

Microbiology study group to Japan

Scientific delegation to Denmark and Finland

Study group for the peaceful use of atomic energy to France

Pharmacology study group to the United States

Scientific delegation to Pakistan

Meteorological inspection group to Japan

Meteorological delegation to North Vietnam

CONFERENCES

Tumor study delegation, Eleventh International Cancer Congress, Italy

Twenty-Sixth Session of the Executive Committee of the World Meteorological Session

International Conference on International Hydrological Decade and on Future Programs in Hydrology (UNESCO-WMO), France

Fourth International Foods Science and Technology Meeting on the Utilization of Sideline Products of Rice in Spain

Thirtieth Annual Meeting, Sri Lanka Association for Advancement of Science

Conference of the World Health Organization

World Food Conference in Italy

World Population Conference in Romania

Source: Foreign Broadcast Information Service (FBIS).

The first category, that of medical teams working abroad, is significant in that it represents the only Chinese groups who have remained out of the country for extended periods and who have actually worked outside China. In 1973, medical teams, periodically replaced by new teams from China, were sent to Guinea, the Yemen Arab Republic, Tunisia, Tanzania, Somalia, Mauritania, Conakry, and Sierra Leone, third world nations whose friendship China wishes to cultivate. In 1974, such rotating medical teams continued to work in Mauritania, Tanzania, and Togo, and a protocol for the dispatch of a Chinese medical team was signed with Senegal in December.

In October 1974, the Chinese sent at least two technical teams abroad, a rice technology group that arrived in Mexico in late October for the purpose of investigating rice cultivation in accordance with a program on cultural, scientific, and technical exchange between Mexico and China, and a Chinese engineering and technical team that arrived in Afghanistan in the same month to assist in the expansion of the Bagrami textile mill. In December, a scientific delegation traveled to Australia and New Zealand.

One other event of 1974 that sheds some light on the state of the social sciences in China was the visit to Japan paid in November and December by a delegation of social scientists from Peking University led by Ma Tzu-ying. The group, which arrived on 12 November and returned to Peking on 6 December, went to Japan at the invitation of the Institute of Humanism of Kyoto University. It was reported that the members of the delegation visited thirteen universities and other academic institutes in Kyoto, Kobe, Osaka, Nagoya, Toyohashi, Tokyo, Sendai, Fukuoka, Naha, and other cities and that they informed members of Japanese educational circles about the "educational revolution at Peking University and how the Chinese people study the history of struggle between Confucian and Legalist schools."[9] That social scientists were reduced to this sort of propagandizing suggests the low level to which their disciplines have fallen in China.

A number of points emerge from the pattern of Chinese visits abroad in 1973 and 1974. One of the most striking is the high degree of Chinese participation in international conferences and in particular the considerable involvement of the Chinese with the World Meteorological Organization and the World Health Organization. Indeed,

---

[9] NCNA, 6 December 1974, Peking.

friendly visits and attendance at conferences in connection with health and medical concerns has been a prominent feature of Chinese activity at the world level.

It should also be noticed that it is with less developed, predominantly third world countries that China has made many of its most active commitments in terms of technical agreements and aid. By contrast, the frequency of visits to the United States has been generally low and the number of scientific missions to the United States declined dramatically in 1974. We can be quite certain that this decline was no accident but rather was a deliberate response to what Peking perceived as delaying tactics on the part of the United States over the question of severing diplomatic ties with the Republic of China on Taiwan.

The frequency of travel abroad during this two-year period varied significantly, not only in relation to the United States. The level of travel abroad was high from May through October 1973 and reached a peak in June 1973. As winter drew on, the number of travelers fell drastically. During early 1974 very few groups of scientists left China. As compared with 1973, the summer months through September 1974 were also very quiet, with only sporadic departures. Beginning in October, however, the number of scientists going abroad began to increase, a tendency that persisted throughout November and December.

These fluctuations in the extent of international participation on the part of Chinese scientists seem to be related to domestic politics. The period from October 1973 to October 1974 during which travel abroad decreased significantly coincided with the high point of a domestic political campaign aimed at criticizing Lin Piao and Confucius. Like most Chinese campaigns of this sort, it was undoubtedly a veiled attack upon a leading political figure. In this instance, the actual purpose of the campaign is believed to have been an attack on Premier Chou En-lai by radical leftists who opposed, among other things, Chou's policy of rapprochement with the West and with the United States in particular. One interpretation of the events of that time is that in the latter months of 1974 Chou succeeded in deflecting the movement to other targets, thus assuring the survival of his moderate position. If this view is correct, the low frequency of Chinese travel abroad during the period before Chou had mastered the movement is readily explicable. This view is substantiated by the rapid increase in foreign travel in November and December 1974, by which time it is presumed that Chou was out of political danger. Whether or not periods of internal political turmoil continue to coincide with periods of decreased international participation on the part of Chinese scientists is another point that will bear watching in the months and years to come.

Internal political conditions may also have been responsible for the generally smaller numbers of foreign vistors to China in 1974 as compared to 1973. While there were visitors to China from the United States throughout the year, they were few in total. It was not until fall, rather than in the summer as one might normally expect, that American visits to China began to pick up again.

In May 1974 American visitors included an acupuncture study group and the physicist Li Cheng-tao, and in June an herbal pharmacology study group and physicist Yang Chen-ning. In July a delegation of the American Medical Association visited China, and in August there were visits by Professor Chang Lin Tien, dean of the Mechanical Engineering Department of the University of California at Berkeley, and by a botanical research delegation. In late August and early September, Dr. Yeh Chien-kuan of the Bechtel nuclear power plant in Los Angeles visited the Atomic Energy Research Institute (CAS) and observed experiments.

September was marked by larger numbers of visiting Americans, including Professor Francis Fan Lee of the Massachusetts Institute of Technology; the astronomer Donald Menzel of Harvard University (emeritus); a group of physicists including Professor Maurice Goldhaber, former director of the Brookhaven National Laboratory, Professor George H. Vineyars, then director of the Brookhaven lab, Professor Robert R. Wilson, director of the National Accelerator Laboratory, Professor Melvin Schwartz, deputy director of the physics department of Stanford University, and Professor Robert Hofstadter, director of the High Energy Physics Laboratory at Stanford University; a seismology study group led by Professor Frank Press, president of the Geophysical Society of America; astronomer Huang Shou-shu of Northwestern University; mathematician Chen Sheng-shen; and physicist Yuen Ron Shen of the University of California. American visitors in October included Professor Jerome B. Weisner, president of the Massachusetts Institute of Technology, and a delegation of linguists led by Professor Winfred Lehmann of the University of Texas, Austin.

In general, however, less can be learned about Chinese interests from the professional associations of Americans visiting China than from the Chinese who go abroad. While some American individuals and groups have been invited to China, clearly because the Chinese wished to have contact with them, a distinction must be drawn between such persons and those who have gone to China under the auspices of the Committee on Scholarly Communications with the People's Republic of China. The composition of these latter delegations is arrived at by negotiation, with the result that they may contain individuals in whom the Chinese have no interest but whom they have had to accept in order to send certain of their own representatives to the United States.

Another way of getting at Chinese interests, of course, is to examine the exhibitions of foreign equipment and technology that have been held in China. For example, in August 1974 two such exhibitions were held, one demonstrating aspects of Swiss industrial technology and the other Swedish biomedical technology. Another exhibition of interest was that mounted by the Germans from 5 to 18 September 1975, which included heavy industrial products, large, heavy, and precision machinery, electronic equipment including laser and maser equipment and transistors, optical products, geophysical and prospecting equipment, and microscopes.[10] Clearly, these reflect some of the more pressing needs of the Chinese in terms of national development.

The record of Chinese participation on the international scientific scene as outlined above provides us with many clues to our future scientific relations, as well as revealing the major factors that affect China's capacity and willingness for interaction at the international level. We can expect these factors to influence both the degree and type of international scientific participation that Chinese scientists will undertake.

Political factors can be expected to exert the greatest influence on the degree of participation. Indeed, internal politics affects not only the extent of international participation in scientific activity but also the quantity of research being done within China itself. The Cultural Revolution, with its attendant disruptions of research and teaching on a huge and unprecedented scale, is the clearest example of this, and, as we have seen, there was a decrease in international travel by Chinese scientists at the peak of the campaign against Lin Piao and Confucius in 1974. Political campaigns of this sort seem to be a recurrent feature of existence in China and appear to be brought about by struggles for power as well as by the need to correct problems within the society.

---

[10] See *Übersee Rundschau*, March 1974, p. 30, for the plans for the exhibition.

Scientists are frequent targets because of the antagonism between them and members of the political sector and because of the strong opposition within the political sector to the creation of a scientific and technological elite of the kind that has emerged in the Soviet Union. It can thus be expected that continuing pressure will be applied to the members of the scientific community to ensure that they remain in their place. It can also be expected that research will be disrupted periodically following phases of political relaxation, as it is found that scientists have slipped away from strictly applied research back to basic studies.

One other domestic political factor of great relevance to international scientific activities is leadership. During the transition from the leadership of Chou and Mao, there is apt to be a time of conflicting views about the importance and desirability of maintaining the international scientific contacts which are part of Chou's handiwork. Much will depend on whether those who finally gain the ascendancy are radical leftists or moderates. At the moment, the influence of the radical leftists is growing, and this could lead to a decrease in scientific contacts with the West and the United States in particular. It is not clear, however, to what extent the leftists perceive continued scientific contact as necessary. This is without doubt the major unknown with which we have to work. It may have considerable effect both on domestic scientific policy and on China's participation at the international level.

The other major political factor affecting scientific cooperation and exchange between China and the United States is international politics. As we have seen, China has undertaken active scientific relations with many Western nations. The glaring exception is the United States, to which very few scientific groups have traveled recently. The decrease in interaction in the sciences closely parallels the fall in the volume of international trade between the two countries from the peak that was reached in 1974.[11] The primary reason for the decrease in scientific activity appears to be the continued American presence in and recognition of the Republic of China, with American disengagement from that country probably proceeding more slowly than Peking originally expected. At any rate, it is clear that scholarly and scientific cooperation between China and the United States is being held at a low

---

[11] The decrease in Chinese purchases from the United States may be the result of the government's having completed the ordering provided for under the current Five Year Plan and may be tied in with problems relating to foreign exchange rather than with internal domestic politics.

level by the Chinese and that this situation can be expected to continue until the problem of Taiwan is solved to Peking's satisfaction. On the positive side, of course, is China's need for the support of the United States as a counterweight to the Soviet Union. However, since scientific and scholarly cooperation does not by itself exert much leverage in dealing with the United States, it seems quite certain that the Chinese will withhold this privilege until it suits their purposes to do otherwise.

If we were to make a prognosis on the prospects for scholarly and scientific exchange and cooperation between the United States and China on the basis of these domestic and international political factors, we would have to recognize that the immediate prospects are relatively poor. For active interchange to occur, the United States will have to cut its political and diplomatic ties with the Republic of China. However, even once this first condition has been met, much will depend on the attitude of the new leadership to promoting cooperative ventures with the United States. Whatever ventures are undertaken will probably be done so from the standpoint of Chinese self-interest and not from any intense desire on the part of the leadership for scientific cooperation in itself. This is not to say, however, that Chinese scientists would not genuinely welcome cooperative studies for purely scientific reasons.

Assuming that all domestic and international political obstacles to cooperative endeavors were swept aside, what would be the prospects for active cooperative efforts? Here again I think they would be limited, unless the Chinese backed away from their policy of using the sciences for primarily utilitarian purposes. We would expect the primary opportunities for exchange to be in those fields to which the Chinese are devoting their major efforts in the service of national development—medicine, the earth sciences, and those biological sciences with agricultural and medical applications. However, because of the emphasis on applied studies in most of these areas in China, joint ventures would have little to offer American scientists working at the frontiers of their fields. Indeed, any scientists who would choose to engage in cooperative studies might do so more out of a desire to assist the Chinese in their national development than out of any hope of solving basic scientific problems.

Thus we should expect cooperative ventures between the United States and China to involve for the most part applied studies, with the American participants working at the practical level in fields like agriculture and public health. In the field of cancer studies, for example, given the Chinese emphasis on prevention and treatment over basic research, one might expect the Chinese government to be more interested in promoting exchanges with American scientists whose primary concern is screening potential anticarcinogenic drugs than with scientists engaged in more basic biomedical studies related to the genetic aspects of cancer.

The intrusion of political influences into the methodological and theoretical aspects of the sciences is another factor that will probably hamper joint ventures and Chinese participation in the work of the international scientific community. Problems of methodology are most likely to arise in the social sciences because of the Chinese ideological antagonism to mathematization and the application of statistical analysis. This might oblige an American behavioral scientist working with a Chinese counterpart to alter his methodological approach for the sake of a joint project. At worst, the methodological differences might result in joint ventures involving only Americans whose orientation to their fields is primarily political. Whatever the field, they would also stand in the way of publication in the most reputable international scientific journals. At the higher level of theoretical interpretation, the Chinese scientist would find himself excluded from serious collaboration with any Western scientist of stature as long as dialectical materialism remained his philosophical creed.

At the individual level, the probability is extremely low that even under optimum domestic and international political conditions a Western-trained Chinese scientist of stature would be permitted to reside in the United States for any length of time. One would expect only the younger and consequently better politically indoctrinated scientists to enjoy such a privilege. Again, one might expect increasing contact between Chinese and American scientists to lead to continuing efforts at indoctrination and reeducation of scientists.

The other side of the coin, of course, is the possibility that a particular American scholar through his writings or actions might become persona non grata to the People's Republic of China. Although this fate is more apt to befall social scientists and humanists, and China scholars in particular, than scientists, it could, at the outside, scuttle an otherwise acceptable cooperative arrangement in the sciences.

Thus, many obstacles stand in the way of full scholarly and scientific exchange between the United States and the People's Republic of China. At this juncture, we cannot be sure when and if further joint research projects, such as those that took place shortly after the visit of former President Nixon to China, will be undertaken, nor do we know what restrictions might be placed on them. In this latter connection, the Chinese may well follow the pattern adopted by the Soviet Union, where American scholars in a number of fields have not been welcome and where difficulties have been particularly severe for social scientists as compared to scholars in "nonpolitical disciplines."[12]

In summary, then, we can expect scientific relations between the United States and China to proceed slowly and to be subject to many vicissitudes arising from both the international political scene and the domestic Chinese political scene. The Chinese will, in effect, make smooth scientific relations contingent upon smooth diplomatic relations. It also seems likely, as has been the experience so far, that opportunities for American scientists to work in China will open up considerably before Chinese scientists will be permitted to reside in the United States for extended periods. We should continue to work toward fostering scientific and technicial cooperation and exchange with China with patience and with understanding of the varied and complex political obstacles that may threaten these endeavors from time to time.

---

[12] *U. S. Scientists Abroad: An Examination of Major Programs for Nongovernmental Scientific Exchange* (Washington, D. C.: U. S. Government Printing Office, 1974), pp. 134–35.

Selected Bibliography

Books

Cheng, Chu-yuan. *Scientific and Engineering Manpower in Communist China, 1949–1963.* Washington: U. S. Government Printing Office, 1965.

Chin, Robert, and Chin, Ai-li. *Psychological Research in Communist China: 1949–1966.* Lexington, Mass.: M.I.T. Press, 1969.

China: Science Walks on Two Legs. New York: Discus Books, 1974.

Gould, Sidney H., ed. *Sciences in Communist China.* Washington: American Association for the Advancement of Science, 1961.

Sidel, Victor H., and Sidel, Ruth. *Serve the People: Observations on Medicine in the People's Republic of China.* Boston: Beacon Press, 1973.

Suttmeier, Richard P. *Research and Revolution: Science Policy and Societal Change in China.* Lexington, Mass.: Lexington Books, 1975.

Watkins, Ralph W., ed. *Directory of Selected Scientific Institutions in Mainland China.* Stanford, Cal.: Hoover Institution Press, 1970.

Articles

Bolt, B. A. "Earthquake Studies in the People's Republic of China." *EOS,* vol. 55, no. 3 (1974).

Chao, E. C. T. "Contacts with Earth Scientists in the People's Republic of China." *Science,* vol. 179 (9 March 1973), pp. 961–63.

Cheatham, Thomas E., Jr. "Computing in China: A Travel Report." *Science,* vol. 182 (1973), pp. 134–40.

"China: Science on a Swing Pendulum." *C and EN,* 6 March 1972, pp. 17–21.

Cooper, Gene. "An Interview with Chinese Anthropologists." *Current Anthropology,* vol. 14, no. 4 (October 1973), pp. 480–82.

Djerassi, Carl. "The Chinese Achievement in Fertility Control." *Bulletin of the Atomic Scientists,* June 1974, pp. 17–24.

Esposito, Bruce J. "The Politics of Medicine in the People's Republic of China." *Bulletin of the Atomic Scientists,* December 1972, pp. 4–9.

91

_____. "Science in Mainland China." *Bulletin of the Atomic Scientists*, January 1972, pp. 36–40.

Han, Suyin. "How China Tackles Cancer." *Eastern Horizon*, vol. 13, no. 6 (1974) pp. 6–12.

Jen, C. K. "Mao's 'Serve the People' Ethic." *Science and Public Affairs*, March 1974, pp. 15–25.

Martin, Charles M. "China: Future of the University." *Bulletin of the Atomic Scientists*, January 1971, pp. 11–15.

Murphy, Charles H. "Mainland China's Evolving Nuclear Deterrent." *Bulletin of the Atomic Scientists*, January 1972, pp. 28–35.

Sidel, Victor H., and Sidel, Ruth. "The Delivery of Medical Care in China." *Scientific American*, vol. 230, no. 4 (April 1974), pp. 19–27.

Signer, Ethan, and Galston, Arthur W. "Education and Science in China." *Science*, vol. 175 (7 January 1972), pp. 15–23.

Tien, H. Ti. "China's Institute of Biophysics and Other Scientific Institutions." *Eastern Horizon*, vol. 13, no. 5 (1974), pp. 39–55.

Tsu, Raphael. "High Technology in China." *Scientific American*, vol. 227 (1972), pp. 13–17.

"U. S. Team's Long Look at China's Agriculture." *RF Illustrated*, vol. 2, no. 2 (March 1975), pp. 1 and 4.

Yang, C. N. "C. N. Yang Discusses Physics in People's Republic of China." *Physics Today*, November 1971, pp. 61–63.

Yee, Albert H. "Psychology in China Bows to the Cultural Revolution." *APA Monitor*, vol. 4, no. 3 (March 1973), pp. 1 and 4.

Cover and book design: Pat Taylor